SNAPSHOT OF SUSTAINABLE DEVELOPMENT GOALS AT THE SUBNATIONAL ADMINISTRATION LEVEL IN CAMBODIA

JULY 2024

ADB

ASIAN DEVELOPMENT BANK

© 2024 Asian Development Bank
6 ADB Avenue, Mandaluyong City, 1550 Metro Manila, Philippines
Tel +63 2 8632 4444; Fax +63 2 8636 2444
www.adb.org

Some rights reserved. Published in 2024.

ISBN 978-92-9270-801-6 (print); 978-92-9270-802-3 (PDF); 978-92-9270-803-0 (e-book)
Publication Stock No. TCS240358
DOI: http://dx.doi.org/10.22617/TCS240358

The views expressed in this publication are those of the authors and do not necessarily reflect the views and policies of the Asian Development Bank (ADB) or its Board of Governors or the governments they represent.

ADB does not guarantee the accuracy of the data included in this publication and accepts no responsibility for any consequence of their use. The mention of specific companies or products of manufacturers does not imply that they are endorsed or recommended by ADB in preference to others of a similar nature that are not mentioned.

By making any designation of or reference to a particular territory or geographic area in this document, ADB does not intend to make any judgments as to the legal or other status of any territory or area.

Corrigenda to ADB publications may be found at http://www.adb.org/publications/corrigenda.

Note:
In this publication, "$" refers to United States dollars.

Cover design by Edith Creus.

On the cover: Various scenes showing progress on SDG achievement across the country at the subnational level (All photos by ADB).

Printed on recycled paper

Contents

Tables, Figures, and Boxes

Acknowledgments

This report was prepared with the technical and financial support of technical assistance (TA) 9387 administered by the previous Governance Thematic Group (GTG) (presently the Public Sector Management and Governance group) of the Asian Development Bank (ADB). The assessment was guided by a framework on Sustainable Development Goals (SDGs) at the Subnational Government (SNG) level prepared by ADB's GTG. Technical guidance and advice were provided by ADB's Rachana Shrestha, senior public sector specialist.

The assessment was undertaken by Kimchoeun Pak, consultant hired under the TA. Farrukh Moriani, an international consultant hired under the TA, provided an initial guidance to Kimchoeun Pak. The assessment team also acknowledges insights and advice from Jhelum T. Thomas, principal public sector specialist, Public Sector Management and Governance Group, ADB, and Chamroen Ouch, senior programs officer (Governance), ADB Cambodia Resident Mission. Additionally, the assessment benefited from the inputs from Rainer Rohdewohld, lead consultant, ADB-TA 9837. The team is grateful for the support and guidance from the Royal Government of Cambodia, and specifically the National School of Local Administration.

Abbreviations

ADB	Asian Development Bank
ASAC	Association of Sub-National Administration Council
BOG	Board of Governors
BSP	Budget Strategic Plan
BSRS	Budget System Reform Strategy
CDB	Commune Database
COVID-19	coronavirus disease
CP	Capital and Provincial
CS	Commune and Sangkat
CSDG	Cambodian Sustainable Development Goals
CSO	civil society organization
DMK	District, Municipality, and Khan
ERW	explosive remnants of war
FMIS	Financial Management Information System
GDP	gross domestic product
ICT	information and communication technology
ISAF	Implementation of Social Accountability Framework
KII	key informant interview
M&E	monitoring and evaluation
MCS	Ministry of Civil Service
MEF	Ministry of Economy and Finance
MEYS	Ministry of Education, Youth, and Sport
MOI	Ministry of Interior
MOP	Ministry of Planning
NAA	National Audit Authority
NASLA	National School for Local Administration
NCDD	National Committee for Sub-National Democratic Development
NGO	nongovernment organization
NPAR	National Public Administration Reform
NPSDD	National Program on Sub-National Democratic Development
NSDP	National Strategic Development Plan
OWSO	One Window Service Office
OWSU	One Window Service Unit
PDP	Power Master Development Plan
PDEF	Provincial Department of Economy and Finance
PFM	public financial management
PFMRP	Public Financial Management Reform Program

SDG	Sustainable Development Goal
SNA	subnational administration
VNR	Voluntary National Review
VSR	Voluntary Subnational Review

Executive Summary

Achieving the United Nations Sustainable Development Goals (SDGs) demands a localized approach. Subnational administrations (SNAs) play a pivotal role since two-thirds of SDG targets are locally oriented. Cambodia, committed to the SDGs through its Cambodian Sustainable Development Goals (CSDGs) framework, faces a challenge as SNAs remain underrepresented in national coordination efforts. This snapshot assessment delves into SNA contributions, encompassing legal and institutional frameworks, budgeting, data and monitoring, and multi-stakeholder engagements. Through diverse methodologies and data collection, this analysis provides strategic recommendations to bolster SNA involvement and SDG localization, thus advancing sustainable and inclusive development.

Despite pandemic-induced setbacks, Cambodia has maintained a robust average economic growth rate exceeding 7%, significantly reducing poverty from 33.8% to 17.8% in the decade preceding 2020. The nation's real gross domestic product growth was projected to rebound to around 5% in 2023. Cambodia seamlessly integrated the SDGs into its national planning system and undertook two voluntary national reviews in 2019 and 2023. Cambodia has initiated various reforms, including decentralization, public financial management, public administrative reform, and judicial reform, aimed at enhancing state capacity and governance. Additionally, reforms in social protection, public safety, and security are underway. Civil society organizations (CSOs) have maintained a crucial role in development, while the private sector and digitalization are reshaping the economy, society, and the public sector.

Cambodia is a unitary state with a democratic parliamentary system, featuring both national and subnational levels. Over the past 2 decades, the governance structure has transitioned from a monarchy to a democratic framework with significant decentralization. The Second National Program on Sub-National Democratic Development, running from 2021 to 2030, seeks to guide these reforms. Recent district-level reforms include restructuring and function transfer for improved efficiency. Multiple stakeholders, including key ministries, development partners, and nongovernment organizations, are actively engaged in the decentralization process.

The study assessed local SDG awareness, revealing limited levels among surveyed individuals, except for those affiliated with CSOs. While Cambodia is dedicated to achieving its CSDGs, SNAs' contributions have often been overlooked, primarily due to low awareness and a scarcity of necessary data. This complicates comprehensively mapping and quantifying SNA contributions to the CSDGs.

Qualitative research indicates that SNAs have contributed to all CSDGs, but the lack of quantitative data, compounded by limited access, sharing, and use of the existing data, impedes accurate measurement. SNAs are particularly impactful in areas like poverty reduction, health promotion, gender equality, quality education, clean water provision, sanitation, and fostering partnerships. Citizens also expect SNAs to prioritize quality education, peace, justice, strong institutions, decent work, economic growth, and health.

Several recommendations include enhancing SDG awareness through digital means, encouraging greater SNA involvement in CSDG activities, and developing and analyzing SDG and SNA datasets. Legal, policy, and institutional frameworks for SNAs in Cambodia have made progress, but coordination remains vital. Despite increased budget allocations, vertical and horizontal imbalances persist, requiring attention to the functional assignment process. Equally important is the need to build SNAs' capacity to deal with emerging issues. Democratic accountability mechanisms within SNAs need strengthening, along with internal and external audit functions.

In addressing these challenges, recommendations include improved coordination through reform mechanisms, enhanced collaboration between central agencies, clearer links between SNA functions and CSDGs, prioritizing function transfer to district levels, fostering relations between district municipalities and line departments, and streamlining SNA engagement with the private sector.

Introduction

Background and Rationale

Efforts not only at the national but also at the subnational level are needed to achieve the 2030 Agenda for Sustainable Development. The 17 United Nations Sustainable Development Goals (SDGs) constitute the global road map for sustainable and inclusive social and economic development. It has been acknowledged that their achievement depends strongly on local progress, as two-thirds of the 169 SDG operational targets have subnational or local dimensions. Globally, subnational governments or administrations accounted for nearly one-quarter (21.5%) of total public spending in 2020, and for more than one-third (39.5%) of total public investment. Nonetheless, the participation and involvement of subnational administrations (SNAs) in national coordination mechanisms in the Asia and Pacific region is far from satisfactory.[1]

Cambodia has committed to achieving the SDGs by adopting the Cambodian Sustainable Development Goals (CSDGs) Framework for 2016–2030 in 2018. The CSDGs have 18 goals, 88 targets, and 148 indicators.[2] In 2019, Cambodia registered with the United Nations to evaluate the results of the CSDGs through the preparation of the 2019 Voluntary National Review (VNR). In 2022, to reflect the latest developments, especially the coronavirus disease (COVID-19) pandemic and to account for data constraints, the CSDG list was revised. In 2022, Cambodia initiated the Second VNR and completed it in mid-2023.

Despite their important contributions, SNAs in Cambodia have not been given much attention in the CSDG documentation and VNR exercises. Located in Southeast Asia with a population of about 16 million, Cambodia is a unitary state with a parliamentary system. The subnational level includes three tiers: Capital and Provincial (CP); District, Municipality, and Khan (DMK); and Commune and Sangkat (CS). The contributions of SNAs to achieving the Cambodia Millennium Development Goals and subsequently the CSDGs have been recognized.[3] However, in both the CSDG and the VNR documents, limited information is available on the SNAs.

The role of SNAs in achieving the CSDGs should be given more attention, especially as the decentralization reform has gained new momentum after slow progress in the last decade. Decentralization first began in 2002 at the CS level, and in 2008 at the CP and DMK levels. The DMK level was set to become the main tier for service delivery but progress in terms of functional and budget transfer has been slow. In 2021, the government adopted the Second National Program on Sub-national Democratic Development (NPSDD or NP2) in order to accelerate reform.[4]

---

[1] (Organisation for Economic Co-operation and Development/United Cities and Local Government [OECD/ULG], 2022).

[2] In addition to the 17 SDGs, Cambodia adds the 18th goal on "End the negative impact of mines/explosive remnants of war (ERW) and promote victim assistance."

[3] See for instance, (Ministry of Planning [MOP], 2022a) (MOP, 2012).

[4] (National Committee for Sub-National Democratic Development [NCDD], 2021).

The implementation of the functional and resource transfer is among the pressing needs for SNA reform in the next few years. The Second NPSDD re-emphasizes shifting functions and budgets to SNAs, especially at the DMK level. Even so, various institutional and human resource constraints remain, preventing SNAs from actively and meaningfully contributing to the National Strategic Development Plan (NSDP), which is linked closely with the CSDGs.[5]

Purpose and Scope

The following steps are recommended with a view to assessing the status of localization—the process of taking into account subnational contexts in the achievement of the 2030 Agenda—of the SDG at the SNA level:

- Gain a better understanding of the challenges, successes, initiatives, and dynamics impacting the localization process, employing methodological pluralism for field research and ensuring consistent engagement with relevant stakeholders during the process.
- Present strategic recommendations for the path toward improving the quality, pace, and relevance of localization of the SDGs at the SNA level in Cambodia.

The resulting diagnostic report is aimed at assisting Cambodia, the Asian Development Bank (ADB), and other stakeholders to sharpen their focus on key dimensions of localization and to address gaps for achieving better results at SNA level.

Conceptual Framework

This report uses ADB's Conceptual Framework for Country Snapshot of SDG Localization in Asia and the Pacific as a foundational document. In response to the 2030 Agenda, ADB continues to step up support for the SDGs in line with its Strategy 2030. The ADB Strategy, Policy, and Partnerships Department initiated the SDG Country Implementation Snapshots in 2019. These snapshots aimed to provide a systematic review of country priorities, gaps, and challenges.

Using the conceptual framework, four dimensions of "Localizing SDGs" are examined:

- **Legal and institutional frameworks of SNAs**, including their legal mandates, organizational structures, and their involvement in national SDG coordination and reporting mechanisms, and capacity development. This will also include planning and programs—whether or not they are coherent across all government tiers and includes CSDG-related indicators in the planning documents.
- **Budget and financing**, to take stock on what budgeting and financing arrangements are in place (including domestic resource mobilization and inter-governmental fiscal transfers).
- **Data and monitoring efforts**, to explore whether data collection and monitoring efforts consider subnational efforts and which local SDG data and monitoring initiatives exist, e.g., local monitoring and evaluation (M&E) frameworks, local data collection, or voluntary local and subnational reviews.
- **Multi-stakeholder engagements, partnerships, and knowledge solutions** to determine whether a whole-of-government approach and collaboration across and at all levels of society is applied.

---

[5]   (World Bank, 2022b).

The findings should help determine whether an enabling environment is in place to allow SDG localization in an effective and efficient manner and what the challenges are. Findings and observations will be relevant for both sector-based interventions and public sector management (PSM) reform initiatives. This approach complements well the basic structure of the SDG Country Implementation Snapshots, which focus on key issues such as institutional architecture and governance; planning, programs, and budgets; financing; and data and monitoring. At the same time, it aligns with ADB Strategy 2030, which stresses the need, among others, for system-wide alignment, enhanced local governance, as well as multi-stakeholder and partnership collaboration in moving forward.[6]

Methodology and Data Collection

The report employs methodological pluralism, entailing collection of data through various means; use of multiple instruments; and triangulation of data, insights, and perspectives obtained during the fieldwork and desk research. This includes:

- **Policy reviews:** These include relevant and latest policies on decentralization reform, (especially the Second NPSDD), public financial reforms, SNA personnel reform, and related sector reform documents.
- **Literature reviews:** Relevant and latest research studies on CSDG, broader macroeconomic development, decentralization reforms, local governance, and development have been collected and reviewed to document what is already known and the specific gaps that this Snapshot can contribute as value addition.
- **Key informant interviews (KIIs) with national-level actors:** With an introduction from the Ministry of Interior (MOI) and in close collaboration with the National School of Local Administration (NASLA), interviews were organized with key stakeholders. These were important in terms of understanding the macro policy environment for the CSDGs. The KIIs were conducted between April 2022 and August 2022, and between April 2023 and May 2023.
- **KIIs with SNAs and line departments:** KIIs covering SNAs and line provincial officials were conducted in four provinces, each representing the four zones of the country, in which five DMKs and five CSs were selected to represent urban, semi-urban, and rural areas. In each SNA, specific respondents were selected to represent different groups and voices, including councilors, the Board of Governors (BOG), and technical officials.

Three online surveys were conducted. They were 1) citizen survey (sample of 207); 2) a survey with SNA officials (sample of 142); and 3) civil society organization (CSO) survey (sample of 170). Figure 1 shows the sample of the three surveys conducted between April 2022 and August 2022.

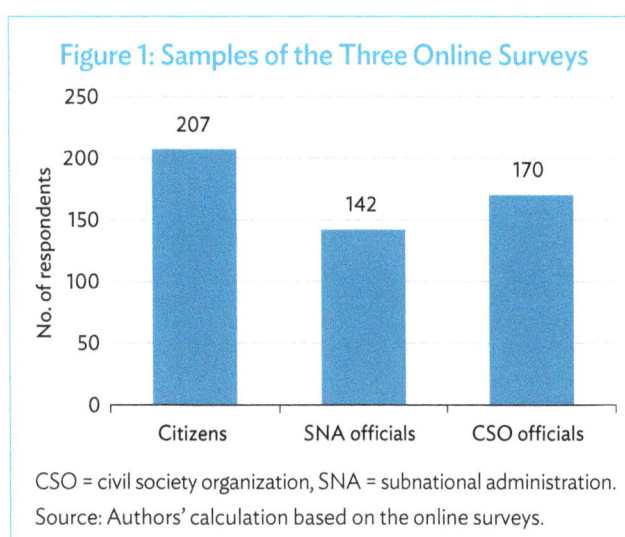

Figure 1: Samples of the Three Online Surveys

CSO = civil society organization, SNA = subnational administration.
Source: Authors' calculation based on the online surveys.

The report is structured to provide information on different aspects of SDG localization and the roles of SNAs in Cambodia. Section 2 presents the broader context of the SDG localization in Cambodia, including the broader socioeconomic development and decentralization reform in the country. Section 3 discusses the findings from the fieldwork on the awareness of SDGs at the local level and the contribution of SNAs to the achievement of key SDGs. Section 4 analyzes the four dimensions of local SDGs at the subnational level: 1) legal, policy, and institutional frameworks; 2) budgeting, functional assignment, and planning at SNAs; 3) accountability mechanisms, M&E, and data work; and 4) multi-stakeholder engagements, partnerships, and knowledge solutions. Conclusions and recommendations are provided in Section 5.

The Context of Sustainable Development Goal Localization and Subnational Administrations in Cambodia

Sustainable Development Goals in Cambodia

Cambodia is a small country in Southeast Asia with a rapid rate of urbanization. It covers an area of 181,035 square kilometers (km^2), categorized into the central plain, Tonle Sap, coastal, and plateau area. According to the latest census conducted in 2019, the country has 15.5 million people, an increase of about 2 million over the past 10 years. About 51% of the Cambodian population are female. The urban population was around 6.1 million in 2019, a considerable increase from 2.6 million in 2008. With rapid urbanization, the share of the urban population rose from 19.5% in 2008 to almost 40% in 2019.[7]

Cambodia has localized the SDGs and integrated them into the national planning system. The SDGs were localized in the Cambodian context in the CSDG Framework 2016–2030. The framework was approved by Cambodia in late 2018 and integrated into the national planning system, especially the NSDP. In addition to the 17 SDGs, the CSDGs have Goal No. 18, which is "End the negative impact of mines/explosive remnants of war (ERW) and promote victim assistance" (Table 1).

Table 1: Cambodian Sustainable Development Goals

Goals	Description
Goal 1	End poverty in all its forms everywhere
Goal 2	End hunger, achieve food security and improved nutrition and promote sustainable agriculture
Goal 3	Ensure healthy lives and promote well-being for all at all ages
Goal 4	Ensure inclusive and equitable quality education and promote lifelong learning opportunities for all
Goal 5	Achieve gender equality and empower all women and girls
Goal 6	Ensure availability and sustainable management of water and sanitation for all
Goal 7	Ensure access to affordable, reliable, sustainable, and modern energy for all
Goal 8	Promote sustained, inclusive, and sustainable economic growth, full and productive employment, and decent work for all
Goal 9	Build resilient infrastructure, promote inclusive and sustainable industrialization, and foster innovation
Goal 10	Reduce inequality within and among countries
Goal 11	Make cities and human settlements inclusive, safe, resilient, and sustainable
Goal 12	Ensure sustainable consumption and production patterns

continued on next page

---

[7]   (National Institute of Statistics [NIS], 2020).

Table 1 *continued*

Goals	Description
Goal 13	Take urgent action to combat climate change and its impacts
Goal 14	Conserve and sustainably use the oceans, seas, and marine resources for sustainable development
Goal 15	Protect, restore, and promote sustainable use of terrestrial ecosystems, sustainably manage forests, combat desertification, and halt and reverse land degradation and halt biodiversity loss
Goal 16	Promote peaceful and inclusive societies for sustainable development, provide access to justice for all and build effective, accountable, and inclusive institutions at all levels
Goal 17	Strengthen the means of implementation and revitalize the Global Partnership for Sustainable Development
Goal 18	End the negative impact of mines/explosive remnants of war and promote victim assistance

Source: (MOP, 2022b).

Cambodia has done two VNR rounds and revised some of the CSDG indicators and targets. In 2019, Cambodia registered with the United Nations to prepare the VNR. With the Ministry of Planning (MOP) playing the coordinating role, another VNR was completed in 2023. Also, in 2022, a revision was made to the list of indicators and targets due to data limitation problems (Appendix 1). In the 2018 CSDGs, there were 18 goals (including 1 national goal), 88 targets (compared to 169 global targets), and 148 indicators, including 96 national indicators (compared to 232 global indicators). After revision, the 2022 version of the CSDG has 18 goals, 95 targets (up 7) and 185 indicators (up 37).[8]

Socioeconomic Context

Macroeconomic Performance

Overall, Cambodia's economic performance in the last decade has been impressive, leading to a noticeable reduction in poverty. Strong economic performance and healthy public finances are the foundation to achieve the CSDGs. In the decade prior to 2019, the average economic growth rate was above 7%. It was brought down to −3.1% in 2020 due to the coronavirus disease (COVID-19) pandemic but was expected to bounce back from 2021 onward.[9] The strong economic performance significantly contributed to poverty reduction from 33.8% to 17.8% over the 10-year period to 2019–2020[10] (Figure 2 and Figure 3).

Although the economy was hit hard by the pandemic, the damage was mitigated by prior policy measures. The collapse of the tourism sector and the initial fall in demand for manufactured goods had contributed to the recession in 2020 and slow growth in 2021. Large fiscal buffers provided room for increased spending on health care, cash transfer to households, and employment support. Even so, the spending pressures compounded by the weaker tax revenue resulted in a larger fiscal deficit in 2021.[11]

Despite the economic slowdown, the recovery was underway in 2021 and continued into the foreseeable future. Gross domestic product (GDP) growth is forecast to be around 5.3% in 2023, as the tourism sector shows signs of recovery.[12] At the same time, public finances are also expected to improve. The fiscal deficit was

---

8   (MOP, 2022a).
9   (MOP, 2022b).
10   (World Bank, 2022a).
11   (International Monetary Fund [IMF], 2022).
12   (ADB, 2023).

Figure 2: Annual Economic Growth, 2012–2023
(%)

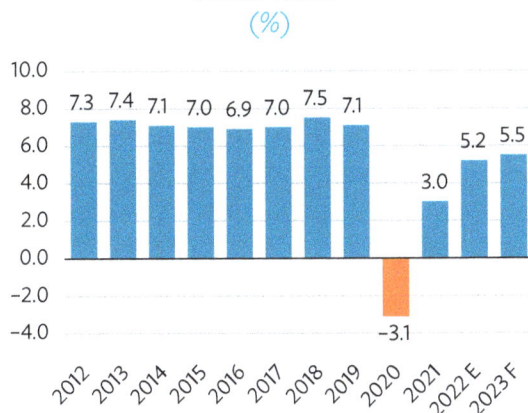

E = estimate, F = forecast.
Source: (World Bank, 2023).

Figure 3: Poverty Trends, 2009–2019
(%)

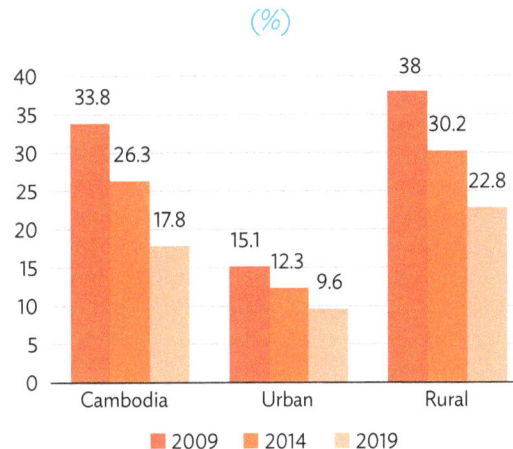

Source: (World Bank, 2022a).

narrowed to around 4% of GDP in 2022 but was expected to increase to 5% in 2023 before falling thereafter to 3% of GDP in the long run. Debt-carrying capacity remains vulnerable to further shocks to exports and growth. However, overall, the increase in the ratio of total public and publicly guaranteed debt to GDP is relatively modest, suggesting that Cambodia is still at low risk of external and overall debt distress (Table 2).[13]

Table 2: Key Macroeconomic Performance Indicators for Cambodia

Selected Indicators	2017	2018	2019	2020	2021	2022 E	2023 F
Inflation, consumer prices (%)	2.9	2.5	1.9	2.9	2.8	5.5	2.5
Revenue (% of GDP)	21.9	23.8	27.0	23.8	22.0	23.2	23.4
Expenditure (% of GDP)	22.7	23.4	25.5	28.8	29.1	29.8	28.9
Overall fiscal balance (% of GDP)	−0.8	0.4	1.5	−4.9	−7.0	−4.7	−5.5
General govt debt (% of GDP)	30.3	28.3	28.1	36.1	36.1	36.7	35.6
External public debt (% of GDP)	29.7	28.5	27.9	33.9	35.1	...	...
Current account balance (% of GDP)	−9.7	−8.9	−15.2	−12.4	−42.6	−26.3	−19.3
FDI, net inflows (% of GDP)	12.1	12.6	13.2	13.5	12.6	12.6	13.5

E = estimate, F = forecast, FDI = foreign direct investment, GDP = gross domestic product.
Source: (World Bank, 2023).

The temporary ups and downs aside, limited diversification remains a weakness of Cambodia's economy.
A few industries have been drivers, especially garments, tourism, and more recently, construction and real estate. The agriculture sector, essential for the economy and rural livelihoods, has consistently experienced the

---

[13]   (IMF, 2022).

lowest growth rate. Micro, small, and medium-sized enterprises have also been underdeveloped.[14] Cambodia has well recognized these challenges and put out short-, medium-, and long-term measures, ranging from skills development to export promotion.[15]

Governance Context and Relevant Reforms

Overall, the governance context not only determines a country's ability to achieve SDGs but also shapes the ability of SNAs to contribute to the endeavor. Governance is defined broadly as the exercise of economic, political, and administrative authority to manage a country's affairs at all levels. The public sector is a key actor, but engagement from non-state actors is also important.[16] In Cambodia, governance forms the core of the Rectangular Strategy Phase IV (currently replaced by the Pentagonal Strategy Phase I),[17] with an emphasis on state reform, effectiveness, transparency, and accountability.[18]

Progress in governance in Cambodia has been mixed. From the government side, through its political platforms, documents such as the Rectangular Strategy Phase IV and high-level development policies such as the NSDP for 2019–2023 place governance at the core of its reform priorities.[19] On the other hand, according to various global rankings, Cambodia's governance is characterized as weak, plagued by poor accountability and uneven progress.[20] Occasionally, there have also been alleged cases of rights abuse and harassment of members of civil society who are seen as not "friendly" to the government.[21] While there is no recent comprehensive assessment, the strong performance by the government during the pandemic and some recent research suggests that it has taken public sector reform seriously, with key ministries such as the Ministry of Economy and Finance (MEF) taking the lead.[22]

Decentralization reform needs to be complemented by other institutional programs to be effective. These other programs include especially the Public Financial Management Reform Program (PFMRP), the National Public Administrative Reform (NPAR), and judicial reforms (Box 1). Two critical relevant points are worth mentioning here. First, the three reforms are critical for improving state capacity and the situation of the whole government. Second, they are supposed to directly complement the decentralization reforms. In a later section, we will look at how such complementarity has been realized in implementation.

A few other relevant governance contexts and reforms deserve more attention, especially in relation to SNAs and SDGs. With peace and stability, Cambodia has become safer for both its citizens and businesses, despite some remaining issues around urban safety, traffic accidents, and drug abuse.[23] The government has also put out the Policy on Safe Communes and Villages, which focuses on key safety issues such as theft, robbery, human trafficking, domestic violence, and traffic accidents.[24] As discussed later, SNAs are at the forefront of implementing this policy.

---

[14]   (World Bank, 2020).
[15]   (Royal Government of Cambodia [RGC], 2021c).
[16]   International Centre for Parliamentary Studies. Governance. https://www.parlicentre.org/about-us/area-expertise/governance.
[17]   (RGC, 2023g).
[18]   (RGC, 2019a).
[19]   (RGC, 2019a) (MOP, 2022b).
[20]   See for instance (Kaufmann and Mastruzz, 2020).
[21]   For a recent example, K. Narim and E. Sea. 2023. Three Detained CCFC Staff Face 10 Years Imprisonment on Plotting, Incitement Charges. *CamboJANews.* 22 May. https://cambojanews.com/three-detained-ccfc-staff-face-10-years-imprisonment-on-plotting-incitement-charges/.
[22]   (The Asia Foundation [TAF], 2022).
[23]   (Global Road Safety Facility, 2021) (MOP, 2022b).
[24]   (RGC, 2021b).

Box 1: The Public Financial Management Reform Program, National Public Administrative Reform, and Judicial Reform

The Public Financial Management Reform Program (PFMRP) is particularly relevant to subnational administration (SNA) planning and budgeting. Started in 2004, the PFMRP seeks to transform Cambodia's public financial management into a decentralized and result-based system by improving budget credibility, financial accountability, policy-budget linkage, and performance accountability. In 2019, in line with the broader PFMRP, the government adopted the SNA Budget System Reform Strategy (SNA-BSRS), which indicates a clear road map and milestones on how SNA budgeting can be further improved and decentralized. The key areas covered by the SNA-BSRS include 1) capital and provincial budget strategic plan; 2) budget preparation, negotiation, and approval; 3) budget execution and monitoring; 4) reporting system, monitoring, and evaluation; and 5) enabling infrastructure.[a]

The National Public Administrative Reform (NPAR) is relevant to SNA personnel management and service delivery. The reform seeks to transfer the public sector into an effective and reliable service provider and partner by focusing on three areas: public service delivery, human resource and institutional management and development, and pay reform. Although the current phase of the NPAR commenced in 2015, it is a continuation from the previous round of public administrative reform which started in the late 1990s. Since 2016, a major policy has been adopted on the management and development of human resource at SNA, which gave way to the adoption of key legal documents on SNA personnel.[b]

The judicial reform agenda seeks to ensure justice for all through improved and more effective judicial services for all citizens. Key reform areas include legal reforms, more effective handling of cases through court systems, and promotion of out-of-court conflict resolution by local authorities.

[a]   (MEF, 2019).
[b]   Those include the Law on Separate Statute for Personnel at SNA (2016); Sub-decree #240 on the Delegation of Authority to Capital, Provincial and Municipalities in Managing Personnel Working at Sub-national Level (2017); Sub-decree #114 on the Organizational Structure and Positions in Line Ministries and Sub-National Administration (2017); and Sub-decree #192 on the Establishment of National School on Local Administration (2016).

Source: (RGC, 2022c).

The second is on social protection, especially social assistance for vulnerable households. This study, as confirmed by other recent reports, finds that, especially since the COVID-19, the government has ramped up social assistance by delivering significant cash transfers to poor households.[25] The research also found that the government, through the National Social Protection Policy Framework 2016–2025, has concrete plans to strengthen the country's social protection system.[26] As will be discussed later, SNAs have played important roles implementing social assistance schemes and other aspects of the framework.

The roles of CSOs and their space constitute another aspect of the broader governance context. CSOs have strongly contributed to Cambodia's development especially since 1993. This study, however, found that the sector has come under pressure both externally and internally during the last 5 years. Externally, key informants from CSOs note that, although they still can engage with the government, the space has become more sensitive politically. Internally, more CSOs have faced funding issues due to overall decrease of donor support and staff shortage partly because of employment competition from the private sector and the government.

---

[25]   (UN Development Programme, Australian Aid, MEF, 2021).
[26]   (RGC, 2016).

Reflecting the country's development trajectory, the private sector has played an increasingly important role in Cambodia. Policy-wise, attracting foreign direct investment (FDI), promoting exports, and developing SMEs have become more central to the government's economic agenda. Implementation has been uneven, however, in the last 5 years. The government has adopted new laws and regulations on investment and SMEs, and offered financial support to certain types of SMEs. However, the regulatory framework for SMEs is limited, along with human resources and vocational skills.[27]

Finally, digitalization has transformed Cambodia's economy, society, and the public sector. Of Cambodia's 16 million population, as of January 2022, there were 13.44 million internet users and 12.60 million social media users. The number has kept increasing, with more uptake of e-commerce and e-payment.[28] From the policy side, the government has adopted the Policy Framework on Digital Economy and Society (2021) and the Digital Government Policy (2022).[29] Key information interviews (KIIs) detail how the government is also in the process of developing a policy framework on data governance. As will be discussed later, digitalization and data governance have become more relevant for SNAs and their contribution to the SDGs.

Decentralization and Subnational Administrations in Cambodia

Overview of Decentralization and Subnational Administration Structures

Cambodia is a unitary state, divided into national and subnational levels. The country has a democratic structure based on a parliamentary system. At the national level, as of 2020, the executive branch consists of 39 ministries that also manage their provincial line departments; 28 public administrations of establishments; 13 state enterprises; and the National Bank of Cambodia. The subnational level has three tiers, including CP, DMK, and CS levels. Through 2019, line ministries also had technical offices at the DMK level. However, since 2019, those technical offices have been integrated into DMK administrations in line with the concept of unified administrations (Figure 4).

Figure 4: Administrative Structure of the Government of Cambodia

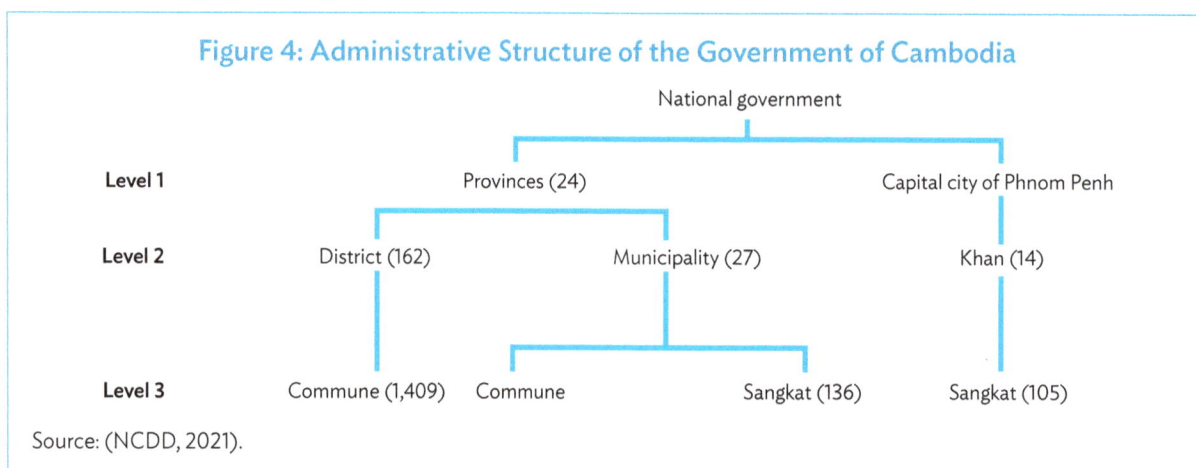

	National government	
Level 1	Provinces (24)	Capital city of Phnom Penh
Level 2	District (162) Municipality (27)	Khan (14)
Level 3	Commune (1,409) Commune Sangkat (136)	Sangkat (105)

Source: (NCDD, 2021).

---

27   (MOP, 2022b).
28   (Datareportal, 2023).
29   (RGC, 2021a) (RGC, 2022a).

The current SNA structure is the result of more than 20 years of decentralization reform and a long history of centralization. Since its independence in 1953, the country's political regime has evolved from a monarchy to a communist state and, most recently, a democratic political structure. Scholars agree that, throughout this historical evolution, centralization has been a constant feature for all the regimes.[30] Since 2002, the government has embarked on decentralization, starting first at the CS level with direct election and, in 2008, at the DMK and CP levels, with the indirect election. Each CS is governed by a democratically elected council, whereas the CP and DMK administrations have an indirectly elected council and a Board of Governors (BOG).[31]

Decentralization has been considered an integral part of broader governance reform, along with the PFMRP, NPAR, and judicial reform (discussed above). Since 2002, a series of policies and strategies have been adopted to guide the reform. In 2010, the NPSDD (2010–2019) was adopted. In 2021, the Second NPSDD was approved as a guide for the period from 2021 to 2030. The Second NPSDD consists of five components, including 1) Reform Leadership and Coordination, 2) SNA Administrative Structures and Systems, 3) Human Resources Management and Development, 4) Fiscal Decentralization and SNA Planning and Budgeting Systems, and 5) Service Delivery and Local Development Component. It also has two crosscutting issues: 1) Gender Equality, Social Equity, and Inclusiveness Mainstreaming; and 2) Climate Change Vulnerability, Disaster Risk Reduction, and Serious Infectious Diseases. Digitalization of SNA systems and function is also a key priority.[32]

In 2019, after slow progress at the DMK level, the government issued sub-decrees on the restructuring and function transfer for the DMK administration. According to the sub-decrees, the whole DMK administrative structure was redesigned to incorporate all the line offices and their personnel (Figure 5).

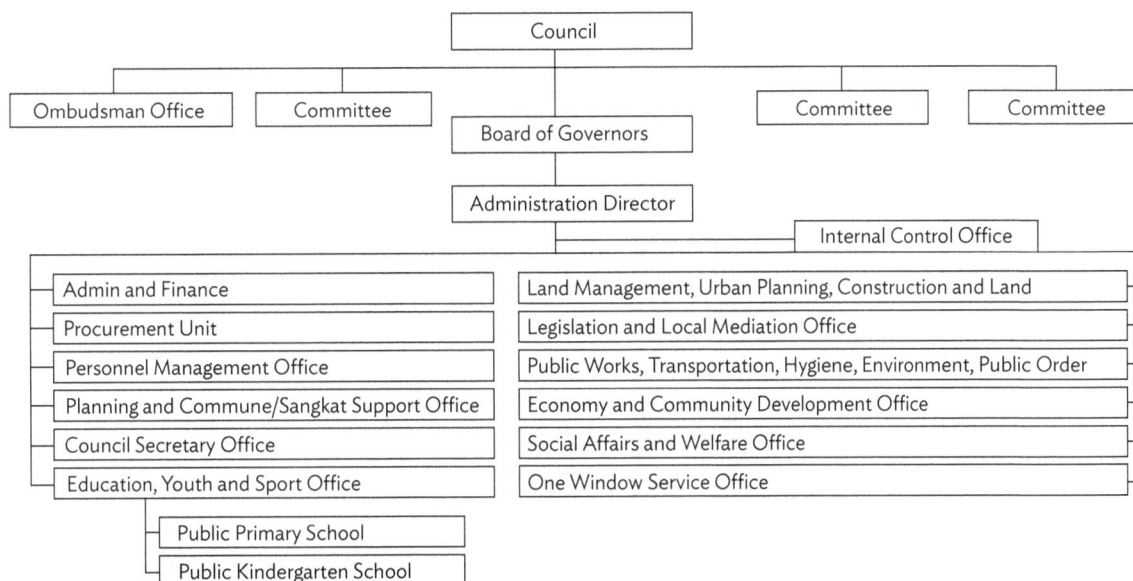

Figure 5: The New Municipal Administrative Structure

Source: (RGC, 2019b).

---

[30]   (Roberts., 2003).
[31]   For a comprehensive discussion about the latest situation and development of SNA governance in Cambodia, please see (World Bank, 2022b).
[32]   (NCDD, 2021).

In addition, a substantial number of functions and technical staff were also transferred, at least in the legal framework. The DMK Councils' administrative remit received transfers of 55 functions, 162 sub-functions, and 278 activities, along with all technical offices and staff members. Under the new structure, new offices were established, combining two or more original line offices. For instance, the former line offices of rural development, agriculture, industry, and handicrafts, mining, and energy and water resource management have been integrated into the Office of Economic and Community Development. The transferred offices and personnel are accountable to the DMK administrations.

The 55 transferred functions cover a range of social and economic sectors which can be linked to the SDGs. These include education, health, agriculture, environment, labor, and others (Table 3). Based on the transferred functions alone, it can be argued that the DMKs are expected to contribute directly to the achievement of the SDGs, for there is much overlap between them and what the administrations are supposed to do. However, as will be argued throughout this report, the main challenge is how the transferred functions get effectively implemented by the DMKs, which is in turn predicated on the clarity of functional transfer, resource transfer, and other related accountability mechanisms.

Table 3: Functional Transfer to the District, Municipality, and Khan Level in 2020

No	Sector	Functions	Sub-functions	Activities
1	Land Management, Urban Planning, Construction	4	9	
2	Rural Development	4	6	
3	Water Resources and Meteorology	3	5	
4	Environment	5	6	26
5	Mines and Energy	3	5	
6	Agriculture, Forestry, and Fishery	5	10	33
7	Public Works and Transport	2	7	
8	Industry and Handicraft	2	3	
9	Commerce	3	4	
10	Tourism	2	10	
11	Social Affairs, Veterans, and Youth Rehabilitation	8	8	32
12	Women Affairs	1	3	
13	Labor and Vocational Training	2	5	
14	Cults and Religion	1	6	
15	Culture and Fine Arts	2	16	13
16	Posts and Telecommunications	1	6	
17	Health	1	8	
18	Education, Youth, and Sports	6	45	174
Total		**55**	**162**	**278**

Source: (RGC, 2019b).

Key Stakeholders

Decentralization reform in Cambodia, as in other countries, is a political process, involving many actors at both the national and subnational levels. At the national level, we have the National Committee for Sub-National Democratic Development (NCDD) which is the coordinating body; core ministries such as the MOI, MEF, Ministry of Civil Service (MCS), and MOP; and all key technical line ministries. Development partners and nongovernment organizations (NGOs) have contributed both financial and technical support to the reform process and SNAs. NASLA and the Association of Sub-National Administration Council (ASAC) have also played increasingly important roles.[33]

---

[33]   See Appendix 3 for a more detailed description of key national stakeholders.

Awareness, Progress, and Contribution of Subnational Administrations to Cambodian Sustainable Development Goal Implementation

Awareness of Cambodian Sustainable Development Goals at the Local Level

As a part of its fieldwork, the study sought to assess the level of awareness about SDGs at the local level. The three online surveys showed that the level of awareness is limited. Regarding citizens, those who said they have heard about SDGs are mostly students and officials in public organizations. In addition, regardless of their professions, surveyed citizens responded that they know about the SDGs from media and social media, especially Facebook. Similarly, surveyed SNA officials and CSO officials also said they got their knowledge about the SDGs from media and social media, although they also point out their regular work, official training, and meetings as their other main sources of information (Figure 6).

Figure 6: Level of Perceived Awareness About Sustainable Development Goals

Q: Have you heard about SDGs?

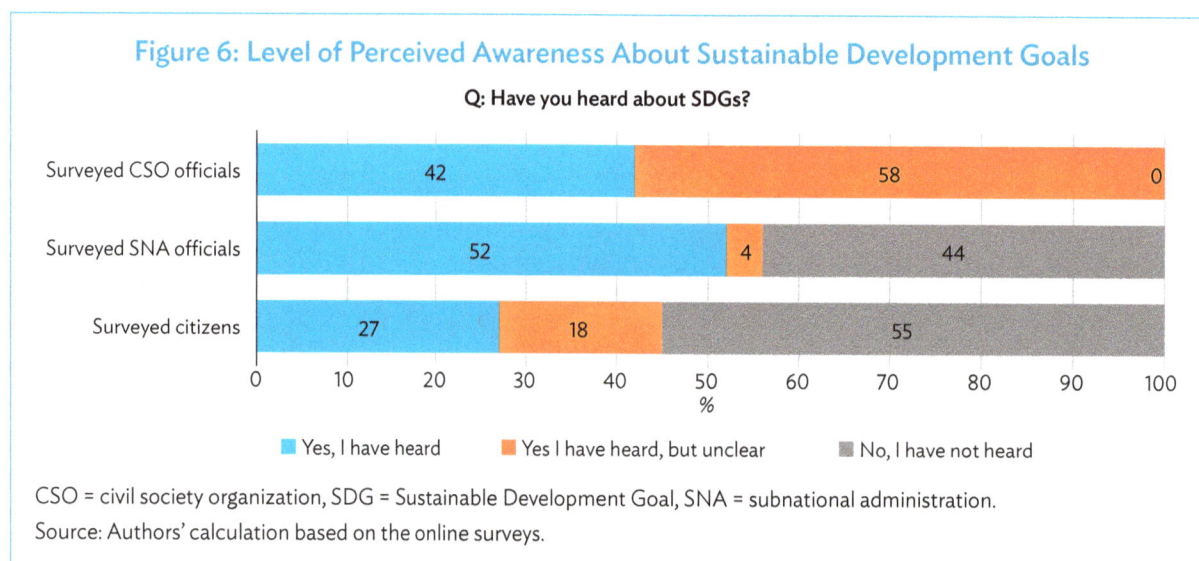

CSO = civil society organization, SDG = Sustainable Development Goal, SNA = subnational administration.
Source: Authors' calculation based on the online surveys.

From the citizen survey, a fair percentage of respondents know about SNA development works. As indicated in Figures 7 and 8, among those who had heard about the SDGs, about 70% said they know something about what SNAs have done, and about 25% said they do not know or refused to answer. Interestingly, there is a high percentage of citizens who said they were either satisfied or very satisfied with how SNAs had handled the COVID-19 crisis. From the survey, it was found that SNAs played crucial roles in raising awareness, enforcing social distancing measures, motivating local residents to get vaccinated, coordinating logistics for vaccination staff, and delivering emergency packages to vulnerable families.

Figure 7: Citizens' Knowledge About Subnational Administrations Development Work

Q: (For those citizens who had heard of SDG) How much do you know about development works of your SNAs?

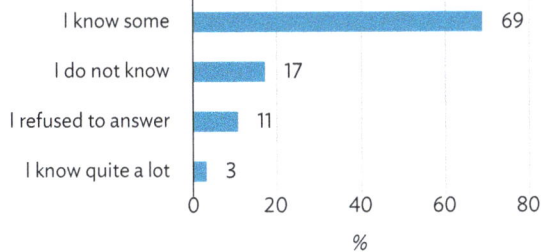

	%
I know some	69
I do not know	17
I refused to answer	11
I know quite a lot	3

SDG = Sustainable Development Goal, SNA = subnational administration.

Source: Authors' calculation based on the online surveys.

Figure 8: Citizens' Perception About Subnational Administrations' Handling of the COVID-19 Crisis

Q: (For those who had heard of SDG) How would you rate the performance of your SNA in dealing with the COVID-19 crisis?

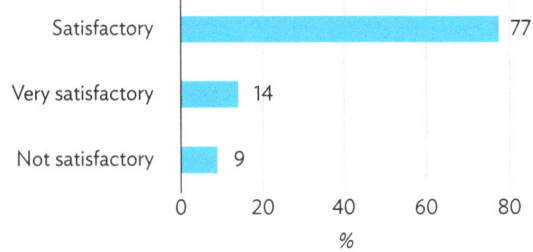

	%
Satisfactory	77
Very satisfactory	14
Not satisfactory	9

COVID-19 = coronavirus disease, SDG = Sustainable Development Goal, SNA = subnational administration.

Source: Authors' calculation based on the online surveys.

The study, through its online survey, assessed key respondents' perceptions on the performance on SNAs. Because of citizens' general limited knowledge, the questions were addressed only to SNA officials (i.e., a form of self-assessment) and to those from NGOs. In defining the sectors, the study uses the categorization currently used for SNAs: infrastructure, social, security and safety, and environment and climate change. As Figures 9 and 10 show, there are no noticeable differences between the perceptions of the two groups. However, combined with qualitative information, it seems that social services and environment have more room for further improvement. The findings, however, should be taken as tentative and be interpreted in conjunction with more qualitative insights, which this report will present in the rest of its discussion.

Figure 9: Perception of Performance by Subnational Administration Officials

SNA survey: How would you rate SNA performance on the following sectors?

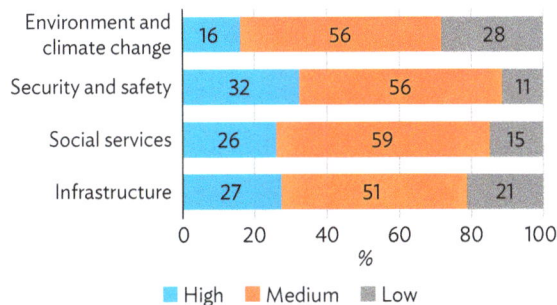

Sector	High	Medium	Low
Environment and climate change	16	56	28
Security and safety	32	56	11
Social services	26	59	15
Infrastructure	27	51	21

■ High ■ Medium ■ Low

SNA = subnational administration.

Source: Authors' calculation based on the online surveys.

Figure 10: Perception of Performance by Nongovernment Organization Officials

NGO survey: How would you rate SNA performance on the following sectors?

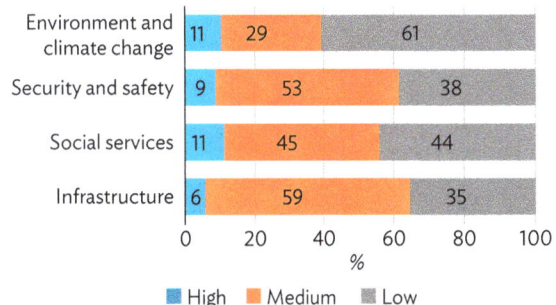

Sector	High	Medium	Low
Environment and climate change	11	29	61
Security and safety	9	53	38
Social services	11	45	44
Infrastructure	6	59	35

■ High ■ Medium ■ Low

NGO = nongovernment organization, SNA = subnational administration.

Source: Authors' calculation based on the online surveys.

Surveyed SNA and CSO officials see a high relevance between SDGs and the roles of SNAs in Cambodia. After presenting the 17 SDG goals, for instance, all surveyed SNAs respond that they are relevant to their work and how they should perform it. Respondents from both SNAs and CSOs also indicated the former have, to different degrees, contributed to the achievement of these goals. Both groups of respondents shared similar understandings about the SDGs that SNAs have contributed to achieving (Table 4).

Surveyed citizens also express their opinions as to what SNAs should focus on. As Figure 11 shows, a large percentage of citizens point to quality education as a key issue that SNAs should focus on, followed by peace, justice, and strong institutions; decent work and economic growth; and health. This finding, however, needs to be cautiously interpreted, given that a high percentage of the online survey participants are youth and those working in the education sector. However, as will be discussed, literature review and KIIs also reveal that SNAs, in the short and medium term, need to pay attention to education (along with other social services) and local economic development, including the issues of jobs.

Table 4: Perceived Areas of Contribution by Subnational Administrations to the Sustainable Development Goals

Ranking	Responses by SNAs	Responses by CSOs
1	Reducing poverty	Reducing poverty
2	Promoting health and welfare	Promoting health and welfare
3	Promoting gender equality	Promoting quality education
4	Promoting quality education	Promoting gender equality
5	Promoting clean water and hygiene	Promoting social equality
6	Promoting partnership	Promoting partnership

CSO = civil society organization, SDG = Sustainable Development Goal, SNA = subnational administration.

Source: Authors' analysis based on the online surveys.

Figure 11: Citizens' Perception on Which Sustainable Development Goals Be Given Priority by Subnational Administrations

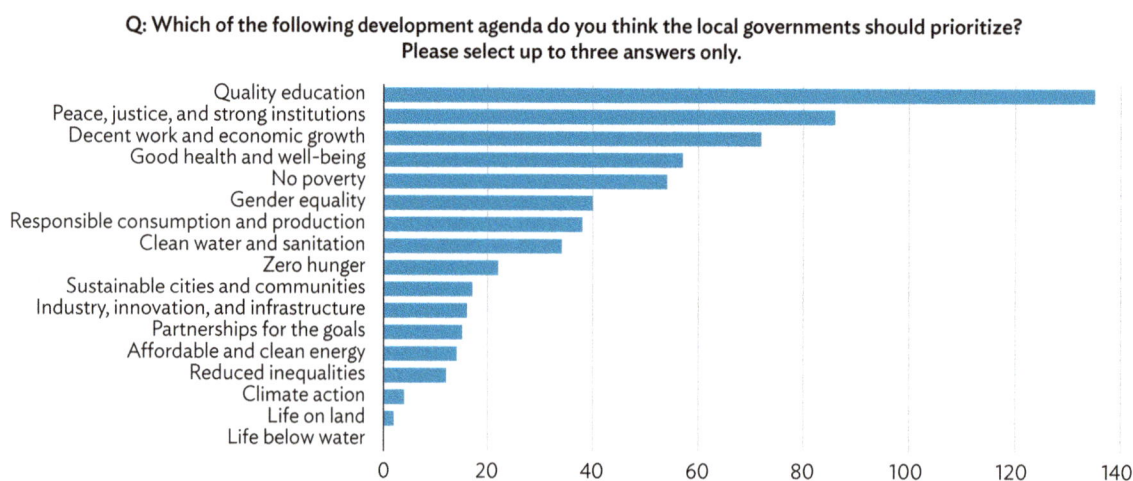

SDG = Sustainable Development Goal, SNA = subnational administration.

Source: Authors' calculation based on the online surveys.

Latest Progress of Sustainable Development Goals and Relevance of Subnational Administrations

This section provides a summary of the latest progress in implementing the CSDGs and contribution by SNAs. On the overall CSDG progress, the study is based on the 2023 CSDG VNR.[34] On the contribution of SNAs, the findings are based on the qualitative information collected from KIIs and latest research reports including the recent Voluntary Subnational Review for Cambodia.[35] There have not been quantitative data that can help quantify SNAs' contribution to CSDG implementation. In a later section, the issues of data and M&E will be singled out as a key gap in the current institutional setup.

An Overview of Cambodian Sustainable Development Goal Progress and Key Activities by Subnational Administrations

According to the 2023 VNR, Cambodia is on track for over 70% of the 185 indicators. As summarized in Figure 12, CSDGs 10, 11, 12, 14, and 7 have all their indicators on track as of 2022. However, about 20% are off track, especially for CSDGs 9, 13, 8, and 2. Missing data is still an issue for at least eight CSDGs.

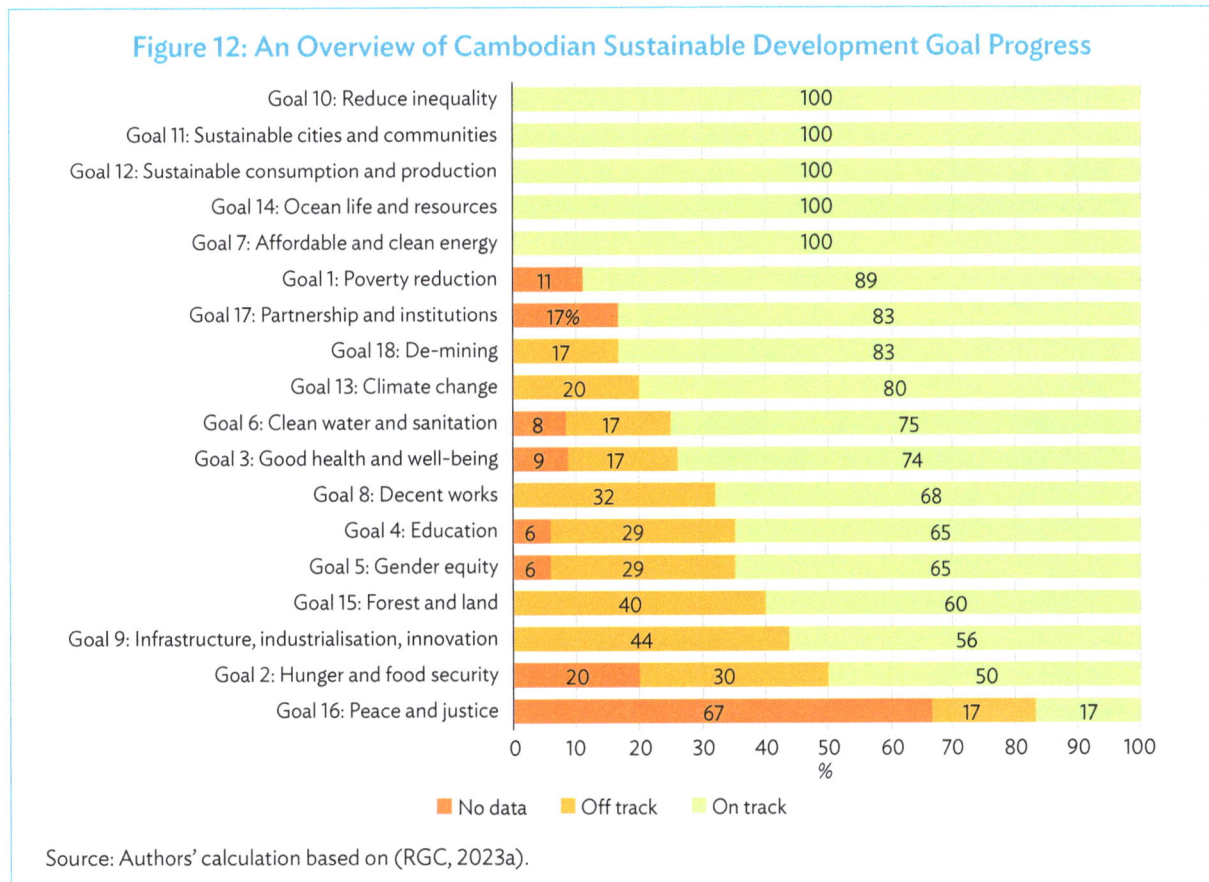

Figure 12: An Overview of Cambodian Sustainable Development Goal Progress

Source: Authors' calculation based on (RGC, 2023a).

---

34 (RGC, 2023a).
35 (ASAC, 2023).

SNAs have contributed to the achievement of the CSDGs through various actions. These range from investing in infrastructure to providing social assistance to vulnerable people to licensing local businesses (Table 5). However, as detailed in the next section, their contribution has not been well documented and quantified. More importantly, they have also been limited by unclear functional assignments and budget constraints.

Table 5: Key Activities of Subnational Administrations to Contribute to Cambodian Sustainable Development Goal Implementation

CSDGs	Activities by SNAs
CSDG 1, 2 and 10—Poverty, hunger, and reduced inequalities	• Supporting vulnerable groups in their communities • Implementing social assistance schemes • Working through the CCWC and WCCC
CSDG 3—Health and well-being	• Contributing to the health centre management committees • Working through the CCWC and WCCC on public awareness, support to pregnant women and children • Vaccination campaigns (include COVID-19)
CSDG 4—Quality education	• Implementing pre-school and child protection works • Contributing to School Support Committee • Working with youth volunteers to support communities
CSDG 5—Gender equality	• Increasing women in the councils and SNAs • Working through the CCWC and WCCC, including on gender-based violence
CSDG 6—Clean water and sanitation	• Improving in rural clean water supply infrastructures • Promoting awareness on hygiene, sanitation, and use of toilet • Implementing works on waste management
CSDG 8, 9—Decent works, economic growth; infrastructure development	• Maintaining security and peace to allow for economic activities • Investing in rural infrastructure, especially roads • Implementing pilot projects on local economic development • Providing administrative services/ licensing to SMEs
CSDG 11, 12—Sustainable cities and communities; Responsible consumption and production	• Implementing functions on urban solid waste management (including on the use of plastic) • Implementing spatial planning in selected areas
CSDG 13, 7—Climate change; sustainable energy	• Collecting data needed for the calculation of vulnerability index and conducting vulnerability reduction analysis • Implementing pilot projects on climate change adaptation • Expanding electricity supplies in the rural area • Implementing pilot projects on solar energy
CSDG 14, 15—Life below water; Life on land	• Implementing functions on sewage system management • Licensing of fishing activities (through OWSU)
CSDG 16—Peace, justice, and strong institutions	• Ensuring public safety and security • Fighting corruption in local service delivery • Conducting out-of-court conflict resolution
CSDG 17—Partnerships for the Goals	• Building partnership with CSO and the private sector • Gradual adoption of e-government initiatives
CSDG 18—De-mining	• Providing information about locations with mine and ERW • Contributing to the clearance efforts by providing local knowledge, mobilizing local people • Providing assistance to mine/ERW victims and their families

CCWC = Commune Committee on Women and Children, COVID-19 = coronavirus disease, CSDG = Cambodian Sustainable Development Goal, CSO = civil society organization, ERW = explosive remnants of war, OWSU = One Window Service Unit, SMEs = small and medium-sized enterprises, SNA = subnational administration, WCCC = Women and Children Consultative Committee.

Source: Authors' analysis based on key informant interviews.

Cambodian Sustainable Development Goal 1, 2, and 10—Poverty, Hunger, and Reduced Inequalities

The 2023 VNR cites decreasing poverty, hunger, and inequality between 2014 and 2019. The report mentioned the poverty rate declining from 26.3% to 17.8% over 2014–2019. The COVID-19 pandemic increased poverty by 2.8 percentage points, indicating that around 460,000 people have fallen below poverty income thresholds.[36] According to the Cambodian Socioeconomic Survey 2021 report, the pandemic has also widened the gap between rich and poor people in Cambodia.[37] For CSDG 2, COVID-19 also increased the prevalence of undernourishment from 6% to 6.3% over 2019–2020, reversing the steady decline of 8.5% which had occurred during 2015–2017.[38]

The study finds that SNAs have actively contributed to reducing inequality by supporting vulnerable groups in their communities. They have done so in at least four areas. First, SNAs, especially the CS level, have been very instrumental in the implementation of the so-called ID Poor program to identify poor households eligible for government and development partner support.[39] Second, they have been at the forefront when implementing the various social assistance schemes, especially during the COVID-19 period. Third, despite limited resources, SNAs, through their women and children committees, have been explicitly tasked to watch out for and support vulnerable families and people in need. The committees have also been engaged in the planning and budgeting process, although their actual influence has been limited. Finally, SNAs have been key partners working closely with various NGOs who deliver services to local people, especially those in desperate needs.

The challenges, however, are the unclear functional assignments and limited resources faced by SNAs, especially for social services. First, at the policy level, based on KIIs at both national and SNA levels, the government still needs to define and categorize better social protection as a function that needs to be performed by SNAs. Once it is defined as a function, it needs to be appropriately costed and funded. Second, in the current situation, insufficient SNAs budgets have been allocated to social services (approximately 6%; please see section on finance).

Cambodian Sustainable Development Goal 3—Health and Well-Being

The VNR highlights key CSDG 3 accomplishments and challenges. The life expectancy of Cambodians of both sexes has increased from 62 years in 2008 to 76 years in 2021–2022, and the quality of life of Cambodians has improved significantly. However, complications of COVID-19 from 2019 to 2022 increased the prevalence of mental illness. In response, social protection schemes, including the National Social Security Fund for Health Care, have been implemented. Health volunteers have also been mobilized during the pandemic.[40]

Document review and KIIs indicate that SNAs' contributions to achieving CSDG 3 have been significant and direct. At the CS level, councilors are permanent and active members of the health centre management committees, which advise, monitor, and hold health centers accountable. The women and children committees of SNAs, especially at the CS level, have also played more roles in supporting people seeking health services (including on HIV-related issues),[41] although their budgets are still very limited (see section 4.2 for more information). SNAs, especially at the CS level, have also been very instrumental in implementing the ID Poor

---

[36] (World Bank, 2022a).
[37] (NIS, 2021).
[38] (RGC, 2023a).
[39] For more information about the ID Poor, please visit: https://mop.idpoor.gov.kh/about/process.
[40] (RGC, 2023a).
[41] (MOI, 2018).

programs and a range of cash transfer and other social assistance schemes initiated by the national-level government and development partners. They have also been the key partners working with health volunteers countrywide.

The reform that will allow for significant contributions of SNAs to CSDG 3 happened with recent functional transfer. In 2019, with Sub-decree No. 193, the government transferred all the responsibilities of the CP Health Department to its administrations.[42] This was a large-scale transfer with the management of all health facilities, staff, and budget expected to be placed under the mandate of the CP administrations who can decide to further delegate down to lower-level SNAs. Despite the progress, however, KIIs indicate that there are many more details to be sorted out to ensure that the intentions of Sub-decree No. 193 can be operationalized and improved over time.

Cambodian Sustainable Development Goal 4—Quality Education

CSDG 4 was flagged in the VNR as one area of success for Cambodia. The progress included improvement in the completion rate at the primary and secondary level, and gender parity. Remaining challenges, however, include the still low rate of transition from primary to lower secondary level, high dropout rates at the lower secondary level, and quality issues virtually at all levels of the education system. As a policy response, the Ministry of Education, Youth, and Sport (MEYS) has adopted the National Education 2030 Road map for CSDG 4, which has 13 different areas of interventions.[43] The VNR also highlights the importance of youth volunteerism in promoting inclusive education and youth engagement in Cambodia.

This study finds that the contribution of SNAs in the CSDG 4 has been noticeable, albeit indirect. In all SNAs, permanent committees and focal persons on women and children's affairs have been set up and appointed, with a broad mandate of addressing various social service issues. At the CS, that committee is the Commune Committee on Women and Children, and at the CP and DMK, it is called the Women and Children Consultative Committee. These committees, especially at the CS level,[44] have been given specific roles to play in delivering various social services, including pre-schools and child protection.[45] Based on the KIIs, local authorities are also involved in the so-called School Support Committee to help bridge the schools and communities.[46] In addition, local authorities have also played key roles in supporting and attracting youth volunteers to work for their communities.[47]

At least up until mid-2023, what prevented SNAs from more meaningfully contributing to CSDG 4 was the limited functional assignment. Education is the most deconcentrated ministry in the government, with more than 90% of its budget and personnel placed under the management of the provincial Department of Education.[48] In terms of functional transfer to SNAs, only limited progress has been made. Functional transfer in the education sector became noticeable in 2016. Since then, however, there have been disagreements on how management over school and teacher salaries should be best transferred to the DMK. As result, in 2019, only administrative tasks performed by Line Offices of Education at DMK were transferred, except for one province, Battambang, where a more significant transfer of pre-school, primary education, and nonformal education has been piloted.[49]

---

[42]   (RGC, 2019b).
[43]   (RGC, 2023a).
[44]   (MOI, 2018).
[45]   (MOI, 2018).
[46]   (World Bank and TAF, 2013).
[47]   Interviews with Voluntary for My Community (VMC) program of MEYS, June 2022.
[48]   (World Bank, 2022b).
[49]   (World Bank, 2022b).

In mid-2023, significant progress was achieved when the three functions were transferred nationwide. According to Sub-decree No. 213 adopted in July 2023, the function for pre-school, primary education, and nonformal education are transferred to the DMK administrations throughout the country, along with relevant finance, state assets, and personnel.[50] The decision was partly based on an assessment conducted by NCDD in late 2022 and early 2023, which indicated specific positive progress after the pilot transfer and how to further improve the management and implementation of those transferred functions in the future.[51] According to Sub-decree No. 213, the DMK administrations are to manage and implement the newly transferred functions starting from January 2024. It remains to be seen how effective the service delivery in these subsectors will be after the transfer.

Cambodian Sustainable Development Goal 5—Gender Equality

Cambodia has made considerable progress toward this goal, with 65% of the indicators meeting their targets. This is particularly true in terms of ending all forms of discrimination against all women and girls, and recognition of unpaid care and domestic works. Women's participation in leadership roles in the government has also seen progress, although not as high as expected. The government plans to address the remaining challenges by emphasizing the national policy on gender: the Neary Rattanak V (2019–2023).[52] The work pertaining to violence against women and sexual and reproductive health is also among key areas for further improvement.[53]

Despite the lack of comprehensive data, this study found that gender mainstreaming and promotion has received much attention at SNAs. First, women have participated in all levels of positions at SNAs, including in the councils, BOG, and as technical officials. As of 2017, 16.8% of all CS councilors were female, 17.5% for DMK, and 17.3% for CP.[54] Women officials at the local level also play active roles in social service delivery, identifying vulnerable households, and preventing and responding to violence against women and children. Women are also said to represent a high proportion of the many youth volunteers working to support SNAs, including a portion of the over 3,000 Community Accountability Focal Persons recruited and working under the Implementation of Social Accountability Framework (ISAF) project. The online survey also found that almost 85% of all SNA officials have attended at least one training on gender equality. At the policy level, gender is considered a crosscutting issue under the Second NPSDD, with a detailed action plan and a periodic gender audit conducted.[55]

The three challenges to promoting gender at the SNAs are lack of budget, data, and capacity. From the KIIs, it is clear that support from other male colleagues and from political parties, while still not optimum, has not been the main issue preventing women from participating in decision-making process at the SNAs. The more constraining factors are the limited budget and human resources allocated to social issues and made available to the women and children committees. Female councilors and technical officials also raise the challenge of timely access to the data relating to their target groups (e.g., vulnerable women and children) and information on referral.

---

[50] (RGC, 2023e).
[51] (NCDD-S, 2023).
[52] (Ministry of Women's Affairs, 2020).
[53] (RGC, 2023a).
[54] Data compiled by MOI (as of May 2021).
[55] (NCDD, 2021).

Cambodian Sustainable Development Goal 6—Clean Water and Sanitation

The 2023 VNR shows satisfactory progress for CSDG 6 despite some limitations. The report shows that, as of 2022, 75% (9/12) of target indicators had been achieved as planned, while 16.7% were offtrack and 8.3% remained without data to assess. This can largely be attributed to the increase in access to improved water sources, both in rural and urban areas. Remaining challenges, however, include 1) lack of the national-level master plan for long-term investment; 2) inability to generate revenue to cover own expenses and investment; 3) limited financial resources for rehabilitation and development of the water and sanitation sector; 4) inadequate technical officers especially at the subnational level to handle the tasks; 5) lack of equipment, materials, and means to implement priority works; and 6) limited citizens' knowledge on the advantages of using clean water.[56]

The contributions of SNAs to CSDG 6 have been limited and indirect. For rural areas, KIIs indicate that although clean water and sanitation have been integral to rural development in general, the budget that SNAs allocated to this sector has been as low as 2% of their total (more budget has been devoted to rural roads). However, their more noticeable contributions have been coordinating the implementation of NGOs and central-level projects. In the urban and fast-urbanizing areas, KIIs indicate that private operators have been playing important roles in service delivery. The challenge is that the relationship and collaboration between SNAs, especially at the DMK and CS levels, have been limited or uneven at best.

As with the cases of other services, one main root cause of the challenges is the limited functional transfer especially to the DMK level. In 2019, the DMK administrations were transferred functions on both rural water supply and sanitation (from the Ministry of Rural Development) and urban water supply (from the Ministry of Industry, Science, Technology, and Innovation).[57] KIIs suggest that, as of now, clear instructions on how both functions should be performed are missing. As with the urban supply, the KIIs indicated that SNAs have had very limited roles in the licensing and monitoring of private operators.

The urban water supply is a good showcase for the importance of SNAs working closely with private operators. Private operators have played increasingly important roles in urban clean water supply in Cambodia. Between 2000 and 2018, approximately 400 private operators financed, developed, and operated water source works, treatment facilities, and distribution networks through a variety of arrangements. However, SNAs have had very limited roles when it comes to this service since, unlike with rural water supply, neither a decentralization pilot nor functional mapping and review were ever done for the urban areas. Also, even after the 2019 transfer, the Ministry of Industry, Science, Technology, and Innovation still follows the 2014 Prakas No. 461[58] when it comes to issuing licenses and monitoring the performance of private operators.

Cambodian Sustainable Development Goals 8, 9—Decent Work; Economic Growth; Infrastructure Development

The progress of CSDG 8 is considerably strong, with 63% of its indicators on track. The impressive economic growth (before the COVID-19), driven largely by the garment, tourism, and construction sectors, was mentioned. Meanwhile, the report also points to specific structural challenges, including the need to diversify and expand its manufacturing base, promote SMEs and local products, formalize the large informal sector, and strengthen tourism. To address these issues, the report mentions several key macro-level policies such as the National

---

[56]   (RGC, 2023a).

[57]   Before 2019, for the rural water supply (under the Ministry of Rural Development), there used to be a pilot of functional transfer, the guideline for which can be found in Prakas No. 161 adopted in 2017.

[58]   (Ministry of Industry, Science, Technology, and Innovation, 2014).

Employment Policy 2015–2025 and the Industrial Development Policy 2015–2025.[59] From the KIIs, it is evident that, in the post-COVID-19 period, the government has placed even more attention on these economic recovery interventions.[60]

Progress toward CSDG 9 is moderate, with just over half of the indicators on track. Successes include infrastructure development, supported by international funds, the adoption of a new investment law, and improved access to communication technology and banking services. However, challenges remain, including limited access to finance and technology, inadequate rural infrastructure, and effects of COVID-19, such as reduced air travel. In response, Cambodia issued various policies and digital frameworks, eased banking regulations, and undertook airport infrastructure projects. However, further policy considerations include diversifying manufacturing, enforcing construction codes, and integrating risk into infrastructure project assessments.[61]

SNAs have contributed to both CSDG 8 and CSDG 9 but their extent is hard to measure. As claimed by all KIIs, SNAs have played important roles in maintaining security and peace, which in turn is the bedrock of economic growth. They have also allocated a large proportion of their budgets (almost 50% in 2021) to local infrastructure investment and maintenance, which is essential for local economic activities. According to the KIIs, SNAs have also played coordinating roles in promoting youth volunteerism and even attracted young people to work as interns and contract staff. However, it is hard to measure how much of these have contributed to overall economic growth and decent work agenda.

Despite the lack of quantifiable data, the study argues that, overall, SNAs' contribution to CSDG 8 has been limited. Three findings emerge from this study to support this argument. First, from the various policy documents, it is mostly the national government mandate which has the explicit roles when it comes to economic policy and economic development. In 2016, the NCDD-S[62] adopted a technical document on local economic development for district and municipality[63] administration. The document defines local economic development as activities that promote cooperation among stakeholders from the public sector, private sector, and civil society. However, the technical document was not a high-level legal document, and its content would need revision in the light of the 2019 sub-decree on functional transfer to the DMK level.[64] Second, the KIIs indicate that SNAs have had very limited roles and responsibilities when it comes to skills development and employment promotion. Document reviews also indicate that functional transfers in labor sector have been very limited.[65]

The third finding is on the limited roles of SNAs in relation to private investment and SME development. First, there is no clear definition as to what investment sizes and types that SNAs should have a role in promoting and regulating. That said, KIIs with SNAs indicate that, on paper, SNAs are entitled to approve any private investment of up to $2 million in capital investment. In practice, however, such roles have hardly been implemented. Most private investment projects have been approved by the national level, with SNAs given only vague "coordinating" roles. Even for these coordinating roles, based on the KIIs, SNAs (including provincial administrations) have not been performing well, partly because they have not been informed and supplied with good data on the various private investment projects operating in their localities.

---

[59] (RGC, 2023a).
[60] (RGC, 2021c).
[61] (RGC, 2023a).
[62] NCDD-S serves as the secretariat for the NCDD.
[63] Khans were not the focus of the technical document mainly because of their different legal and economic conditions of being within the capital of Phnom Penh.
[64] (RGC, 2019b).
[65] Please see for instance (RGC, 2017).

As with SME development, the one area that SNAs have been most involved with is the licensing of business activities through the One Window Service Units (OWSUs) and One Window Service Office (OWSO). The OWSUs, which operate at the CP level, and the OWSO (at the DMK level), are delegated certain business licensing functions, as stated in 2017 Sub-decree No. 18 and subsequent Prakas on the establishment and functioning of one-window service mechanisms at SNAs.[66] The KIIs with SNA officials indicate that, in the last 3 years, CP administrations have received more delegated business licensing functions from line departments, which, in turn, led to substantial increase in OWSU revenue. The revenue is then spent as a part of the annual budget of the CP. The challenge, however, is at the DMK level, where the business licensing authority is still limited to micro businesses, with very low revenue-generating potential. Section 4.2 on planning and finance will discuss more on these questions as a part of SNA nontax revenue question.

Anecdotes suggest that the current legal framework on business registration is not supportive enough for micro and small businesses in the informal sector. Such actors deliver most of the economic activities in Cambodia. The government has made efforts to encourage micro and small businesses to formalize. At SNAs, the tasks fall especially on OWSO at the DMK level, where different types of micro businesses can apply for licenses. While the effort is appreciated, two specific areas according to the KIIs need improvement with CSOs and SNAs, backed up by review of relevant documents: One, while encouraging business registration, the current licensing requirements have rejected those without fixed business addresses, such as mobile and street vendors. There are no exact statistics on the number of such businesses, but they are very common especially in urban and fast-urbanizing areas. With such a requirement for an address, mobile and street vendors have no choice but stay informal. Second, interviews with CSOs suggest that the current business licensing process with OWSOs, while already much simplified, needs to be further streamlined and go online if it is to promote more business registration.

Cambodian Sustainable Development Goal 11, 12—Sustainable Cities and Communities; Responsible Consumption

The VNR focuses mainly on solid waste, wastewater management, and urban spatial planning for CSDG 11. First, it is noted that, for this goal, lack of data is a key challenge, including on solid waste amounts, plastic bags usage, and annual average of the parameters of carbon dioxide, nitrogen dioxide, sulfur dioxide, total suspended particulate, PM2.5, and PM10. Second, the report associates the progress so far with the decentralized management of waste in urban areas. This indicates the expected importance of SNAs in sustainable cities and communities.[67] This study, through its KIIs, confirmed this finding.

CSDG 12 has shown notable progress, with targets met amid COVID-19 challenges. This has been largely due to the Ministry of the Environment commitment to environmental conventions and private sector collaboration on waste management. However, implementation has been hampered by limited public awareness and participation, constrained resources, an underdeveloped regulatory framework, and inadequate private sector involvement and monitoring systems. To boost progress, the Ministry of the Environment is focusing on activities like monitoring public water and air quality, targeting pollution control, and implementing environmental impact assessments.[68]

---

[66]   (RGC, 2017).
[67]   (RGC, 2023a).
[68]   (RGC, 2023a).

In both policies and implementation, SNAs have explicit and critical roles in urban solid waste management. In the newly adopted National Policy on Solid Waste Management (2020–2030), SNAs, especially at the DMK level, are considered as key actors in delivery and management of urban solid waste.[69] In November 2015, Sub-decree #113 on urban and solid waste management was introduced. In Sub-decree 182 and Sub-decree 184, the transfer of solid waste management to DM administration was re-emphasized. Since 2015, selected municipalities have received a so-called "environmental budget."[70] Despite the achievements, however, KIIs indicate that continuous improvement is needed to further clarify and strengthen the roles of DMKs, especially in relation to contractor management, fee collection, and execution of the transferred budget.

Spatial planning is another area through which SNAs have contributed to CSDG 11. According to the 2011 National Policy on Spatial Planning, all SNAs must prepare their land-use planning to facilitate medium- and long-term development process.[71] KIIs suggest that, in major urban areas, CP and DMK administrations, with technical assistance from the Provincial Department of Land Management, Urban Planning, and Construction, have prepared the plans (although no specific number was provided). However, one remaining challenge is how to ensure SNAs can link their socioeconomic planning (i.e., the 5-year Development Plan and 3-year Investment Plan) systematically with their land-use planning.

Cambodian Sustainable Development Goal 13, 7—Climate Change; Sustainable Energy

CSDG 13 progress has been significant, with four of five indicators on track. According to the 2023 VNR, the percentage of communes/sangkats that are vulnerable to climate change dropped from 36.3% in 2019 to 34.2% in 2022 thanks to the government implementation of the Climate Change Strategic Plan, which focuses on building resilience to climate change and disasters triggered by natural hazards. Various strategic plans and measures against climate change, and substantial public expenditure have also been implemented. However, challenges include a lack of funds, COVID-19 disruptions, limited access to technical support, deficient greenhouse gas reduction technology, limited private sector involvement, and insufficient climate change information dissemination. To address these, policies like the Cambodia Climate Change Strategic Plan 2014-2023, Third National Communication, Long-Term Strategy for Carbon Neutrality, and the National Action Plan for Disaster Risk Reduction 2019–2023 have been put into place.[72]

Climate change and disasters triggered by natural hazards affect the functioning of SNAs. According to KIIs, they have worked to assess local vulnerabilities to natural hazards, identify priority needs, and respond quickly to emergencies such as floods and drought. SNAs are also the frontline service providers to the population during disasters triggered by natural hazards. Since 2010, key achievements include the adoption of the vulnerability reduction analysis; awareness raising and capacity development for SNAs on climate changes; and noticeably, the accreditation of NCDD-S as a Green Climate Fund national implementing entity. It was learned from the KIIs that NCDD-S has received support from various donors including the United Nations Capital Development Fund, Swedish International Development Cooperation Agency, United Nations Development Programme, Global Environment Facility, International Fund for Agricultural Development, and ADB for activities related to climate chage. In the Second NPSDD, climate change and disaster management are also considered key crosscutting issues to be implemented in the next 10 years.

---

[69] (RGC, 2021d).
[70] (MEF, 2022a).
[71] (RGC, 2011).
[72] (RGC, 2023a).

Despite the achievements, key structural and capacity challenges remain. Based on KIIs, except for those receiving earmarked funds for climate adaptation activities, climate planning and implementation by SNAs have been very limited. This is also applicable to the DMK to whom specific climate change-related functions were transferred in 2019.[73] KIIs at the national level indicate that, overall, awareness, capacity, and data relating to climate change (e.g., meteorological data) available at SNAs are still too limited to allow for meaningful climate adaptation planning.

As with CSDG 7, the progress has been steady, with all indicators on track. Cambodia's power system has experienced remarkable growth in demand over the past decade. Investments are increasing in the power sector. By the end of 2022, Cambodia issued 471 licenses for electricity distribution, investing, and developing electricity supply networks covering 14,151 villages, accounting for 99.88% of the total number of villages nationwide. Despite the progress, however, about 245 villages are yet to be connected to the electricity grid. The government is working to address these and other challenges through the implementation of various key policies such as the Power Master Development Plan (PDP) 2022–2040, the National Energy Efficiency Policy 2022–2030, and other policies relating to clean energy.

SNAs have contributed to clean energy development but in indirect and limited ways. Cambodia has outlined principles for solar rooftop power, focusing on permit issuance; capacity allocation within the master plan; and transparent, accountable management of installations.[74] According to KIIs, SNAs have contributed to implementation but only indirectly and mainly as facilitators for central government agencies or private companies. They have also contributed to clean energy initiatives through the implementation of solar energy projects in selected communes, with support from donors such as the United Nations Development Programme. NCDD-S has been the main coordination body for such projects.[75]

Cambodian Sustainable Development Goal 14, 15—Life Below Water; Life on Land

The VNR assesses the progress on CSDG 14 as highly satisfactory, and on CSDG 15 as moderately satisfactory. Key achievements include waste management (including plastic), drainage system upgrade, reforestation efforts, and expansion and protection of protected areas. Key challenges remain, including still noticeable levels of illegal fishing; improper waste disposal into the ocean; impact of climate changes; and limited capacity, resources, and decentralization of works relating to these conservation efforts.[76]

SNAs' contributions to CSDG 14 and CSDG 15 have been direct although still limited and unquantifiable. Three specific examples were identified during the field interviews. The first is the decentralization of functions on solid waste management and drainage system management to SNAs, especially urban districts. The transfer was begun in 2015. Another example is the delegation of functions to DMKs with regard to licensing of fishing activities. The third example is the ongoing reform to amend the legal frameworks on fishery, forestry, and protection areas to allow SNAs more authority over these conservation tasks.

The main challenge preventing SNAs from actively contributing to the achievement of these two CSDGs is limited functional transfer and resources. On the one hand, SNAs are expected to ensure proper management of fishery and forestry resources in their localities. They are supposed to be the key partners working with CSOs such as forestry and fishery communities. On the other hand, however, their roles have not been specifically determined, leading to uncoordinated efforts and conflicts with sector line agencies. The lack of functional

---

[73]   (RGC, 2023a).
[74]   (RGC, 2023a).
[75]   Interviews with NCDD-S officials (May 2023).
[76]   (RGC, 2023a).

clarity has been compounded by chronic lack of resources, both financial and human, and unreliable monitoring, evaluation, and data.

Cambodian Sustainable Development Goal 16—Peace, Justice, and Strong Institutions

As a country, Cambodia has been striving to ensure peace, political stability, and social order. Politics aside, these efforts have served as the foundation for economic growth and good governance reforms, including decentralization and justice reforms. Central to these reforms is the building of stronger state institutions that can better serve the people and reduce corruption. The VNR also points out to the progress in terms of freedom of associations and partnership with civil society organizations (CSOs). In all the areas where improvements have been made, the report also recognizes various challenges that can be addressed by improving awareness, access to data, and capacity and resources to enforce the laws.[77]

SNAs' contributions have been significant when it comes to ensuring peace, security, and public order. First and foremost, these are their legal roles as provided in the Organic Law and in the Law on the CS, as well as other key official documents, especially the Policy on the Village, Commune and Sangkat Safety.[78] Through local elections, SNAs, especially at the CS level, have also contributed to peace building by creating political space for people from different parties to work together in the council.[79] Some key informants, especially those outside the government, raised concerns that the abolition of the main opposition party back in 2017 has diminished the political space at the local level in Cambodia.

SNAs have also contributed to better justice and anti-corruption, especially in relation to service delivery. Based on the KIIs, SNAs, especially the CS, have been acting as the out-of-court conflict resolution mechanisms for local people. However, such roles have been limited to only minor conflicts and its implementation effectiveness has been uneven or unknown. Accountability mechanisms have also been put in place to curb corruption in local service delivery, noticeably through the ombudsman office and other complaint-handling mechanisms at all SNAs. SNAs have performed these roles in close partnership with CSOs, a topic to be addressed with respect to CSDG 17.

Cambodian Sustainable Development Goal 17—Partnerships for the Goals

At the national level, the partnership has been achieved through various mechanisms. As indicated in the VNR report, through the implementation of the Development Cooperation and Partnership Strategies 2014–2018 and its successor for the period 2019–2023, Cambodia has managed to mobilize resources to implement CSDGs. The government has also invested in generating and sharing more reliable data to ensure effective development targeting. Partnership with NGOs have also been strengthened, especially through implementation of the Law on Associations and NGOs, which was adopted in 2015.[80] However, key informants, especially those outside the government, raise concerns about the overall shrinking space for NGOs working to promote human rights and advocacy around politically sensitive issues such as land and natural resource management.

Partnerships have been a cornerstone for decentralization reform and SNA functioning. The government has worked closely with development partners to develop and strengthen SNAs' governance structure and fund local development activities. NCDD-S, which is the key body for the decentralization reform, has also

---

[77] (RGC, 2023a).
[78] (RGC, 2021b).
[79] (World Bank and TAF, 2013).
[80] (RGC, 2023a).

been coordinating various donor programs and support.[81] However, as the KIIs revealed, better coordination is needed both among government agencies and donor agencies in supporting sector programs on the one hand, and decentralization reform on the other. For instance, anecdotal evidence suggests that some sector donor projects have been designed without factoring in how all line offices have already been integrated into the DMK administrations since 2019, and that many of the sector functions have already been assigned to this SNA.

At the SNA level, partnership with CSOs have been a common practice, but not yet with the private sector. KIIs and online surveys suggest that partnership with CSOs has continued, although the perception of whether it has gotten better varies by respondents and location. SNA officials interviewed in some locations observed that there have been fewer NGO-funded projects in the last 5 years, but they also maintain that NGOs are still their main partners, especially in the areas of social services, livelihood promotion, and environment protection. Similar observations were also shared by interviewed and surveyed CSO officials. What is most limited is the partnership with the private sector. Despite encouragement at the policy level and significant contribution by the private sector to local development, all SNAs interviewed said they have not had a clear mechanism nor roles when it comes to coordinating with the private sector.

Limited data is one of the main challenges preventing SNAs from effectively coordinating with other stakeholders and developing their planning. First, the KIIs confirm all level of SNAs have virtually no reliable information on private investment and public investment from the national level, both of which constitute a large proportion of investment financing, especially in urban areas. Second, the effectiveness of data storage, sharing, and use has been limited in terms of its contribution to SNA planning exercises. Every year, SNAs are required to collect a large amount of data, some for their own planning purposes (i.e., the 5-year Development Plan and 3-year Investment Programs), and some for uses by national programs (e.g., the ID Poor data). KIIs suggest that planning agencies (especially the Provincial Department of Planning and the Planning and Investment Unit of SNAs) have increasingly had a hard time collecting, compiling, sharing, and putting such data into meaningful uses. Lack of information and communication technology (ICT) infrastructure and capacity explains why much of the data are still kept in Microsoft Word or Excel formats on various computers, vulnerable to data loss, unauthorized changes, or clerical errors.

Cambodian Sustainable Development Goal 18—De-mining

Cambodia, according to the VNR, has made good progress on mine and ERW clearance, although actual achievements to date are generally lower than planned. The country has achieved a major reduction in mine and ERW casualties. In 2020, there were 65 cases reported, while in 2022 there were 44 cases of mine and ERW casualties reported. By the end of 2022, Cambodia had 1,976 km^2 of mine- and/or ERW-contaminated areas, including 649 km^2 of landmine-contaminated areas and 1,328 km^2 of ERW-contaminated areas.[82]

SNAs have directly contributed to CSDG 18, although the extent of their contribution is unquantifiable. First and foremost, they are the ones who identify and provide information about mine and ERW locations. They also contribute to the clearance efforts by providing local knowledge, mobilizing local people, and implementing assistance schemes to mine and ERW victims and their families. However, concerns were raised during interviews that some SNAs still lack capacity in collecting and relaying information about ERW and are not equipped with basic skills on how to respond when faced with specific mine- and ERW-related situations.

---

[81]   (NCDD-S, 2022).
[82]   (MOP, 2023).

The Four Dimensions of Localizing the Cambodian Sustainable Development Goals

This section details the state of localization of the 2030 Agenda at the SNA level in Cambodia. Having presented the latest situation on how SNAs have contributed to the achievement of the 18 CSDGs, the report now discusses how the SDGs have been localized down to the SNA level. It does so by looking at the four dimensions of SDG localization mentioned in the conceptual frame above. These include 1) policy, legal, and institutional frameworks; 2) budget and financing; 3) data and monitoring efforts; and 4) multi-stakeholder engagements, partnerships, and knowledge solutions. From the discussion, the report expects drawing concrete conclusions and recommendations on how the roles of SNAs can be more prominently reflected in the CSDG discussion and how they can be made more effective.

Legal, Policy, and Institutional Frameworks

The legal, policy, and institutional frameworks shape the ways SNAs function and contribute to the achievement of the CSDGs. They define the legal status, roles, and responsibilities of SNAs in relation to the citizens and other stakeholders. They evolve as the decentralization reform progresses from one stage to another. This section starts with the legal framework, followed by the policy and institutional arrangements with relation to SNA reform in Cambodia. In each part, relevance to the CSDGs will be highlighted.

Despite much progress, the legal, policy, and institutional frameworks on SNAs in Cambodia have come to a point where consistency, coordination, and implementation have become critical. The study found that there have been many laws, regulations, and policies which seek to define and reform the organizational structure, functions, resources, partnership, and accountability of SNAs. However, there are still gaps in key aspects, such as on functional assignments, partnerships with the private sector, and monitoring and evaluation. Even more challenging is the consistency and coordination among key laws, rules, and policies. Not addressing these challenges will prevent SNAs from effectively contributing to the national development priorities and, by extension, CSDG achievement will be undermined.

Key Laws and Regulations

The legal framework for Cambodia's decentralized governance and reform is found in various laws and regulations. These range from the Constitution to the Law on Administrative Management of the Communes/ Sangkats (for the CS level); the Law on Administrative Management of the Capital, Provinces, Districts, Municipalities, and Khans (for the CP and DMK levels); and other laws and sub-decrees focusing on specific aspect of SNA governance, including financial management and personnel management.[83]

---

[83] For more information on those specific laws and regulations, please see Appendix 2 and a recent study by the World Bank (World Bank, 2022b).

By mid-2023, at least four new laws were enacted that can have significant implications, especially on financial management. The first is the new Public Finance System Law, which was adopted in 2023. Unlike the 2008 version, the new law has more provisions on the budgets of SNAs, including information comprehensiveness and presentation.[84] The second is the 2022 Law on Non-Tax Revenue, which includes more specific provision on the roles of SNAs in planning, collecting, and managing nontax revenues including those from public services and state assets.[85] The third is the new Law on Procurement (2023), which provides a new legal framework for public procurements where SNAs are considered a type of procurement-implementing agencies.[86] The fourth is the 2023 new Law on Taxation, replacing the 1997 version.[87] Unlike the nontax revenue, SNA roles are not emphasized when it comes tax revenue collection and planning.

These new national-level legal frameworks will serve as the background for revising SNA-related budgeting processes. From KIIs, it was expected that, after the public finance system is adopted, the next step is to revise the 2011 Law on the SNA Finance Regime and Asset Management. The new national public finance law will also provide the framework for revising two important sub-decrees on public budgeting, which also affect the budget control, payment process, and accounting practices at SNA level. Those two sub-decrees are 1) Sub-decree #81 on expenditure control (1995) and 2) Sub-decree #2 on public accounting rules.[88]

While the legal framework has become more comprehensive, specific legal gaps and inconsistencies need urgent attention. With many legal documents adopted and new reform initiatives continuously implemented, more clarifications and adjustments are needed to ensure the new laws and regulations are complete and consistent. For instance, new rules for SNAs need to be adopted to follow the new sub-decree on nontax revenue, internal audits, and state asset management. Similarly, legal clarity is also needed on the classification of obligatory versus permissive functions, along with more technical guidelines on how the DMKs should perform their newly transferred functions.[89]

The legal and regulatory review process can be very time-consuming, which has in turn delayed the implementation of the reform itself. This point relates closely to the DMK level but also to the whole of decentralization reform. According to this, the transferring line ministry needs to revise existing Prakas on how the function should be implemented. In some cases, such as functions that involve fee charging and collection (i.e., nontax revenue), such regulatory changes require not only the line ministry but also the MEF to get engaged. Regulatory changes are time-consuming, which in turn can delay and affect the implementation of the transferred functions.

Legal awareness and compliance at the subnational level is as important. Consistently, key SNA informants acknowledge that there have been many laws and rules to follow and that some officials might not comply with or be aware of them. According to them, a few factors contribute to the challenge. The first is the turnover of SNA officials, ranging from the councilors to technical staff. The second is the absorptive capacity, especially of those in their senior years. The third is the limited effectiveness of the current information-sharing and cascade training approaches. The section on institutional and capacity framework will discuss more on these.

---

84   (RGC, 2023d).
85   (RGC, 2022b).
86   (RGC, 2023b).
87   (RGC, 2023c).
88   (RGC, 1995a) (RGC, 1995b).
89   On new laws and regulations that need to be adopted and revised, please see (NCDD, 2021).

Policy and Strategy Framework

The SDGs are reflected mainly in the decentralization reform policy, but not in a separate policy document. Unlike the national level where there has been effort to explicitly link SDGs to the NSDP, for subnational-level policy, the SDGs are only mentioned once, without any further elaboration on what it means for the SNAs in their performance and contribution. In the newly adopted Second NPSDD for 2021–2030, for instance, the government seeks to ensure that subnational governance and development are carried out in accordance with the national development priorities and the SDGs. Reference to the SDGs is also found in the subnational planning guidelines.[90] Box 2 elaborates the relevance of the second NPSDD to the SDG agenda. In both instances, however, there is no detailed elaboration on what SDGs are and how they can be reflected in the detailed implementation of the reform or in the SNA planning process.

Engagement and awareness by SNAs in the whole SDG agenda, however, has been limited. The KIIs indicated that, since the start of the SDG localization process back in 2015, no direct consultation has been made with SNAs, but only through the MOI and Association of Sub-National Administration Council (ASAC). It would be too time-consuming if such a broad consultation were to be done. This observation is well in line with the survey findings presented earlier about the level of perceived awareness about SDGs among SNA officials, CSO officials, and citizens.

Although not explicitly, the SNA development agenda and the SDGs are connected, at least in indirect ways. First, the SNA development agenda covers four broad sectors: 1) economic development, 2) social development, 3) natural resources, and 4) administrative and public order. These four sectors, in turn, cover eight issues or subsectors, including agriculture, business, education, health, vulnerable groups, environment, security and public order, and gender. There are obviously some overlaps between these sector areas and the 17 SDG targets (as discussed in the above section on CSDG and contribution by SNAs). Second, there has been a recent effort to better link subnational development priorities to those at the national level, which is more explicitly linked to the SDG agenda.

Albeit implicitly, the Second NPSDD is the reform medium through which SNAs can better contribute to the SDG agenda. Only when they are provided with clearly defined functions, allocated following clear, coherent principles (e.g., subsidiarity, the economy of scale); sufficient financial resources (e.g., own sources revenue, national transfer, assets); capable human resource; effective partnership with other non-state actors (including private sector); and impactful M&E mechanisms, can SNAs in Cambodia be expected to effectively promote local service delivery and development. Those expected results will in turn lead to improvement in key SDG areas, be it education, health, energy, natural resources, or urban development.

This snapshot study finds that the main and persistent policy challenge is at the implementation stage. While appreciating the policy frameworks of the government, virtually all the key informants attest that the implementation has been slow and uneven due to several key challenges. Among them, they include limited awareness and compliance of the policies, rules, and regulations at SNA level; limited policy coordination at the national level; limited technical capacity; weak M&E and data use; lack of partnership with non-state actors; and decreasing people participation. All these points are elaborated in the succeeding sections.

---

90   SNA planning guideline (2017) and revised guideline (2020).

Box 2: Relevance of the Second National Program on Sub-National Democratic Development to the Sustainable Development Goal Agenda

Although not explicitly provided, the spirit of the Second National Program on Sub-National Democratic Development (NPSDD) is to promote the roles of subnational administrations (SNAs) in contributing to achievement of the national development priorities and, by extension, the United Nations Sustainable Development Goals (SDGs). Its vision is that "citizens have improved access to public services and benefit from local development provided by the SNAs in a socially equitable and inclusive manner and eventually contribute to achievement of socioeconomic objective in advancing Cambodia to middle high income country in 2030."

To realize the vision, through the implementation of the Second NPSDD, it is expected that SNAs in Cambodia will be better able to implement their expected roles. The Organic Law (2008) provides that SNAs shall establish, promote, and sustain democratic development, which, in turn, includes the following elements: public representation; local autonomy; consultation and participation; responsiveness and accountability; promotion of quality of life of the local residents; promotion of equity, transparency, and integrity; and measures to fight corruption and abuse of power.[a]

The Second NPSDD seeks to strengthen the SNAs by focusing on their structure, functions, resources, and accountability. Different tiers of SNAs are expected to have different focus. For instance, the province administrations, organized as unified regional administrations, would focus more on providing technical support, legal monitoring, and aggregating and coordinating planning for local service delivery, whereas the district/municipal and commune/sangkat administration would focus on direct interaction with citizens and providing needed services to local people.

The Second NPSDD is relevant to the SDGs both in terms of what it expects SNAs to perform and how they should perform those functions. To start off, the program expects the SNAs to play active roles in key sectors, ranging from education, health, water supply, environment, justice, and others. Its emphasis on gender equality, social equity, and inclusiveness also resonates with the SDG's overall spirit of "leaving no one behind." The policy also has climate change and disaster management as crosscutting issue, corresponding directly to the SDG on climate action. Reflecting Cambodia's rapid urbanization, the Second NPSDD singles out the need for urban development and even the plan to develop Phnom Penh Capital Administration into a metropolitan. This speaks directly to the SDG 11 on sustainable cities and communities.

The Second NPSDD expects SNAs to better perform their roles not only through better legal and regulatory framework but also via better use of technology. For instance, the document singles out e-government as one area for urgent attention, which corresponds to the SDG's focus on technology and innovation. In the Second NPSDD, the government expects the SNAs to improve local service delivery and development with state resources and more effective partnership with non-state actors, including private sector. This intention implies a direct connection to the partnership-dimension of the SDGs.

[a]   (RGC, 2008), Article 11, 12.
Source: (NCDD, 2021).

Coordination across reforms has also become more challenging in the last few years. To be effectively implemented, the NPSDD needs to be coordinated with other reforms. Those include the three governance reform programs mentioned earlier: the Public Financial Management Reform Program (PFMRP), National Public Administrative Reform (NPAR), and judicial reforms. Equally important are the various sector reform agendas such as education, health, agriculture, SMEs, social protection, and others. Such cross-reform coordination has been less than satisfactory, resulting in delays in the functional assignment, resource transfers, capacity building, and M&E system development for SNAs.

Policies and reform agendas under sector line ministries also have a direct impact on the implementation of the decentralization, local service delivery, and, by extension, SNAs' contribution to CSDGs. They are particularly relevant to the decentralization particularly with relation to the functional transfer process. Sector policies set out specific programs and subprogram objectives, activities and resources, targets and monitoring, and evaluation frameworks. They might also point out the rules and regulations on how those functions should be performed (e.g., how specific licenses should be issued, technical standard of how a service should be provided, etc.). When some of those activities (or functions) are transferred to the subnational level, their implementation needs to be in line with certain technical standards and contribute to achieving the overall goals set at the national level.

This section points out three other policies that need to work closely with the decentralization to allow SNAs more room to contribute to the CSDGs. The first is the social protection policy. In the last few years, both national and subnational officials recognize that SNAs have played important roles in implementing social assistance schemes. The contribution, as confirmed by KIIs, was especially noticeable during the COVID-19 pandemic. Results from the online survey also confirm this observation, as illustrated in Figure 13. However, based on the interviews with MOI and the National Social Protection Council, the roles of SNAs have not been sufficiently and systematically recognized in the current National Social Protection Policy Framework 2016–2025. For instance, according to the KIIs, provisions on those roles are provided in various task-specific sub-decrees (such as on the ID Poor, on cash transfer pilots, etc.), but they have not been explicitly recognized as a "function" that SNAs should be assigned and accountable for.

Figure 13: Perceived Contributions by Subnational Administrations Regarding COVID-19 Responses

Q: How would you rate the level of constribution of SNAs in addressing COVID-19-related issues?

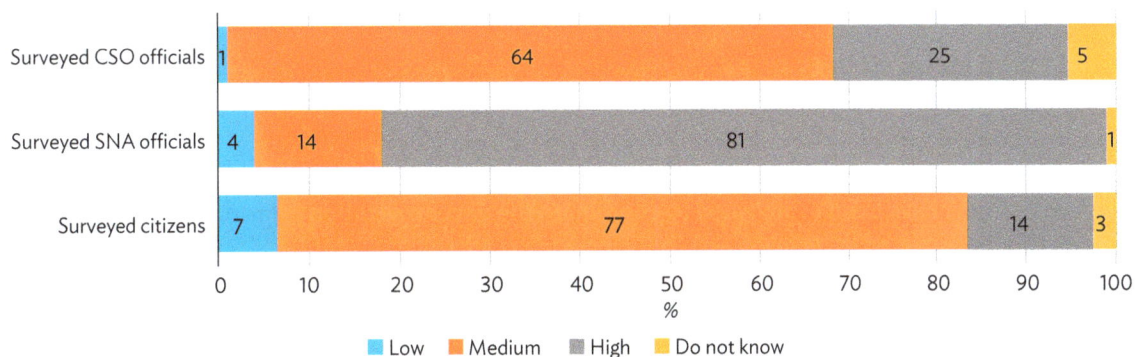

	Low	Medium	High	Do not know
Surveyed CSO officials	1	64	25	5
Surveyed SNA officials	4	14	81	1
Surveyed citizens	7	77	14	3

COVID-19 = coronavirus disease, CSO = civil society organization, SNA = subnational administration.

Source: Authors' calculation based on the online surveys.

Promoting the roles of SNAs in social protection (including during a pandemic period), however, requires more systematic policy considerations. Based on the KIIs with MOI and the National Social Protection Council, a few policy questions emerge. First, the government needs to clearly define social protection (both social assistance and social insurance) as a function to be performed by the public sector, including SNAs. Second, in the language of functional transfer, such functions need to be clearly categorized and, where necessary, differentiated from other social services such as health, education, and child protection. Third, the identified functions to be transferred need to be properly costed to minimize unfunded mandates.

The second set of policies is the one relating to private investment and SME development. The decentralization reform has so far focused on local infrastructure development and, to a lesser extent, social service delivery. In the context of post-COVID-19 economic recovery and long-term plans to transform Cambodia into an upper middle-income country by 2030, it is important that SNAs have concrete and active roles in local economic development. In terms of the linkage to the national-level policies, this means the roles of SNAs should be made more explicit in the implementation and regulation of private investment (both foreign and domestic) and the support for SME development.

SNAs struggle to effectively promote and regulate private investments due to unclear definitions of their roles and lack of data on local projects. As discussed in the above section on the broader context, their involvement is seen mostly in business licensing via OWSU and OWSO. However, the existing legal framework is insufficient for supporting micro businesses in the informal sector. Current licensing requirements reject those without fixed addresses, forcing them to remain informal. Improvements, like further streamlining and digitizing licensing processes, are suggested for better business registration promotion.[91]

The third set of policies is the national policy on e-government. Based on policy review and KIIs, there has been a strong agreement among policymakers, SNA officials, and CSOs that digital technology is critical for improving SNAs' capacity and local service delivery. The Second NPSDD even has e-government as a crosscutting component, with a reference to the national level policy on Digital Society and Economy.[92] In practice, the use of digital technology has been focused on communication, management processes, and data. According to the KIIs, e-government is emphasized in the policy; in reality, it has been very challenging for SNA to request national budget to spend on ICT infrastructure and capacity building. In many cases, when an SNA has initiatives relating to ICT, it must look for support from development partners.

Institutional Framework, Coordination, and Capacity at the National Level

There is no specific mechanism set up at the national level for the SDG subnational-level localization. Instead, as mentioned, the SDG localization process is focused on the national level, with SNA voices represented by the MOI and the ASAC. Because the SDG relevance for SNAs is integrated through the decentralization reform, the coordination is also expected to happen through the existing mechanisms, as discussed. However, from KIIs, in its various meetings, there has been no explicit focus on SDG and SNA.

Various mechanisms have been established to coordinate the decentralization reform, with many central and line ministries expected to be involved. Those include the NCDD, MOI, MEF, MCS, MOP, and sector line ministries. Besides the state actors, non-state actors including development partners, CSOs, and the private sector have also contributed to the reform process.

---

91   For more details on OWSO and OWSU, please see Appendix 4.
92   (NCDD, 2021).

The Second NPSDD recognizes the importance of coordination and leadership. According to the document, leadership of the whole reform program comes from the highest level of government, but effective implementation will need commitment, ownership, and active direction of reforms at the level of ministries and agencies at the national level and from the leadership of the SNAs themselves. Therefore, reform leadership and management do not refer only to the highest level but to leaders in many different agencies and at all levels of government. Reform leaders at all levels, as well as external stakeholders and citizens, need to fully understand the strategic vision and purpose of the reform program. Effective communications to build this understanding are a key element of reform leadership.

This report identifies key progresses in terms of awareness, commitment, and coordination to support the reform. Overall, interviewed officials at both national and SNAs show a higher level of understanding of the decentralization and its importance which, to them, implies less resistance. About 70% of SNAs also replied they know about the Second NPSDD, although the extent and details of their knowledge is not known. That said, KIIs suggested that only officials in the management level were directly consulted when the Second NPSDD was finalized. Time constraints and the limitation regarding in-person gatherings due to the COVID-19 pandemic were raised by the NCDD-S as the main reason.

The MEF has been playing an increasingly active role in the decentralization reform. The adoption of the SNA Budget System Reform Strategy (SNA-BSRS) 2019–2023 was one key accomplishment giving a clear road map for how SNA financial management can be improved. Other key progresses mentioned include the implementation of the program-based budget and the rollout of the Financial Management Information System (FMIS) at the CP level; streamlining and decentralizing specific aspects of SNA budget execution (e.g., procurement and petty cash); improving SNA nontax revenue management, and initiating the discussion on tax revenue for the subnational level. The challenge is to ensure coordinated implementation of the reform actions at all levels with effective feedback mechanisms between the levels of governments, and regular review of both implemented and planned reform actions.

Coordination among key ministries has also seen progress, but many urgent challenges remain. As mentioned earlier, a mechanism for coordinating the main reform programs (i.e., the decentralization, the PFMRP, NPAR, and the judicial reform) has been established. To make it more effective, a concept note on coordination mechanisms has been drafted and discussed in May 2022. Based on the interviews, the effort, which is still at its early stage, has identified many areas that key ministries, especially NCDD-S and MEF, need to discuss and agree upon. Those include the cross-reform coordination itself, SNA budget transfer, own-source revenue, personnel management, state asset management, etc. The most urgent and significant question of all, however, is on functional assignment. As mentioned, disagreement has become clear over to what extent the 55 functions transferred to the DMK are appropriate and implementable.

The MOP has been the key ministry leading the development and improvement of the planning process at the subnational level. The main progress reported include the adoption of key SNA planning guidelines in 2017 and, more importantly, the joint Prakas No. 0149 in 2020 to ensure a coherent timeline between SNA planning and the budget formulation process at both subnational and national level. One remaining challenge, however, is how to ensure all SNAs have the capacity to provide timely data for the preparation of the CP Budget Strategic Plan (BSP). Another challenge is around the use and dissemination of the rich budget and economic data collected every year in each province. In doing these, collaboration across reform programs and among key national agencies is crucial. Another important task to address is how to incorporate spatial planning into SNA planning process.

The MCS has been in charge of SNA personnel management. The key progress to mention was the transfer of thousands of personnel from line ministries to the DMK level following the 2019 sub-decree Numbers 182, 183, and 184, and the broader SNA personnel management policy, laws, and regulations adopted in 2020.[93] The challenge, however, is to ensure that human resources management reflects the new organization structure and accountability lines. In term of capacity building, MCS, which leads the NPAR reform programs, needs to also overcome the coordination challenges in working the other reform programs and agencies.

The study finds that engagement from line ministries, with only a few exceptions, has been limited in pushing the decentralization reform especially at the DMK level. Noticeable progress has been made for education, health, and social affairs in terms of functional and resource transfer. However, the results have been mixed for ministries such as agriculture, rural development, industry, and others. From both national and SNAs interviews, it is confirmed that many of these other ministries have so far focused on transfer of functions to the OWSU at CP level, but not yet on the new service delivery arrangement at the DMK level after the transfer of the 55 functions.

The engagement of sector line ministries has faced three key challenges. The first one is the human resources and capacity of the so-called D&D working group within each ministry. This working group was created since the implementation of the NPSDD and is expected to continue during the next phase, this time called the Steering Committee on Sub-National Democratic Development (SC-SNDD) The interviewees raised the concern about the level of influence, resources, and capacity of the SC-SNDD, compared to the responsibilities it has to offer.

The second challenge is the feedback loop on the progress of the functional transfer. Both central agencies (e.g., NCDD-S, MEF, MOP) and line ministries acknowledge that they have not had a good update on the progress on the functional transfer process, let alone a feedback loop of what has worked and not worked in terms of service delivery as resulting from the transfer. The communication line in the last few years has been particularly difficult due to the COVID-19 crisis, but it has also been caused by systematic weak reporting and data sharing between SNAs and provincial line departments, and between the line departments and their own parent ministries.

The third challenge concerns donor projects, both in their design and implementation. This is particularly relevant to those ministries where donor funding is still channeled through stand-alone projects. Although many sector projects have followed the standard operating procedures to maximize their alignment and harmonization with the government system, interviews suggest that decentralization has not been factored sufficiently in their design. For instance, in one case, a donor project still expects a fishery function to be done by the provincial line department, although such function was already transferred to the DMK. In their implementation, many donor projects are still centralized, with the central project implementation unit in charge of most management, while provincial line departments implement certain tasks, and SNAs hardly get involved. With their large share of funding, these donor projects can have significant impacts in how the decentralization progresses.

---

[93]   Those policy and legal documents include, among others, the Policy on the Management and Development of Human Resources at SNAs (2013); Law on Separate Statute for Personnel at SNAs (2016); Sub-decree #240 on the Delegation of Authority to Capital, Provincial and Municipalities in Managing Personnel Working at Sub-national Level (2017); Sub-decree #114 on the Organizational Structure and Positions in Line Ministries and Sub-National Administration (2017); and Sub-decree #192 on the Establishment of National School on Local Administration (2016).

Another new key actor is the National School of Local Administration (NASLA). NASLA was established in 2016 for "building capacity for civil servants, council of sub-national administrations, students, and other stakeholders as well as conducting research on governance, local development, enhancement of local autonomy and management of sub-national administration." NASLA started providing training programs in 2018 and its role will be even more important, especially for building the capacity of DMK personnel, including the newly transferred personnel. To be effective, however, NASLA needs to recruit new staff, build its capacity, and seek collaboration with capacity-building organizations/institutions, specialist organizations and public/private institutions of higher learning, and professionals to design and deliver training courses. ADB has been a key stakeholder on this front, providing financial and technical support to NASLA through an $11.05 million project that forms part of its support to Cambodia under the Second Decentralized Public Service and Financial Management Sector Development Program. By upgrading infrastructure, improving curriculum, and strengthening staff professionalism, this project will help NASLA become a modern, more efficient, and relevant institution. The project also expects to provide structured capacity building to SNA staff, especially at the DMK level, using both formal training and on-the-job training.

NASLA also has plans to raise awareness among SNAs about SDGs and promote better SNA-related data management, which can be also help SDG implementation. In 2022, with technical support from the United Nations Department of Economic and Social Affairs, NASLA organized the "Training of Trainers Workshop on Effective National to Local Public Governance for SDG Implementation in Cambodia" to strengthen capacity of public institutions in implementing SDGs, especially at the subnational level. After the workshop, NASLA has been developing a more coherent training curriculum for further trainings for SNA officials.[94] Meanwhile, the school also has plans to better manage data relating to SNA development needs, planning, budgeting, and other related governance aspects, and have it stored and shared from a central database. According to NASLA, one immediate need to implement these plans is technical support. However, as will be detailed in a later section, coordination among key stakeholders regarding data management is just as important.

Institutional Framework, Coordination, and Capacity at the Subnational Level

There are no mechanisms explicitly designed for SDGs at the SNA level, although they are mentioned in key SNA guidelines. As already discussed, SNAs are expected to contribute to the SDGs by aligning their development priorities to the NSDP, which is then linked to the SDG at the global level. With this logic, SNAs can contribute to the SDGs only to the extent that it contributes to the NSDP. In addition, the SNA planning guidelines of 2017 and 2020 mention the need for SNAs to align development priorities to the SDGs. That said, field interviews suggest that SNA have only limited knowledge of and engagement with SDG matters, and that the SDGs are only mentioned in passing.

Cambodia, especially MEF, has made significant progress during the last 3 years on linking SNA planning with the NSDP. As guided by the SNA-BSRS, each CP has developed a BSP, which integrates the investment plans and aligns the plans of line departments toward achieving specific development objectives in the four sectors: economic development, social development, environment, and administration and public order. The development of the CP-BSP, however, has just started, with more work to be done to ensure the expected integration.

---

94   Interview with NASLA officials (June 2023).

Awareness of SNA officials about the SDGs and their capacity to implement the new planning process is still limited. As presented earlier, only a little more than 50% of SNA officials said they have heard of the SDGs. SNA KIIs also indicate their understanding is limited regarding the new planning process, which (according to the joint Prakas #0149) requires the CS and the DMK to send their investment plans to the provincial level and then into the CP-BSP before mid-April each year. The interviews also indicate the challenges of data sharing and data use in the current SNA planning process, which will be elaborated in a later section.

Limited SNA capacity has been frequently raised both at the national and subnational levels. Lack of capacity has been a constant concern since the start of the decentralization in 2002, despite the many trainings and capacity-building sessions each year.

In this research, we tried to specify the capacity needs at SNA level and develop some recommendations. Based on the KIIs, the capacity needs include:

- **Information on new working arrangements and procedures**—As a result of ongoing reforms especially in the last few years, new structures and processes have been put in place, especially at the DMK level. SNAs officials expressed the need to be better informed about these changes and how to implement them in their routine works.
- **Specific technical knowledge for performing their functions**—This is applicable to both staff working in supporting units such as investment, planning, budgeting, and personnel; and technical staff working in service-providing units such as the OWSU and OWSO, and technical offices under the DMK administration.
- **Knowledge on new technology**—This includes practical knowledge on how to use ICT such as the FMIS, Non-Tax Revenue Management Information System, and the new digital portals (for DMK and CS levels), and better use of Zoom, Telegram, online surveys, etc.
- **General knowledge**—This covers a range of topics from SDGs (as in this study), to basic concepts on gender, climate change, etc.

This snapshot identifies specific factors leading to the persistent capacity challenges—both at the national and subnational levels. At the subnational level, four factors repeatedly come up. The first is the high turnover among staff members, which requires that new training is done when new persons get recruited. The second is the lack of ICT-related equipment such as computers and reliable internet connection. The third has to do with absorptive capacity of existing officials, especially for new technologies. It was recognized that senior officials, while rich in working experience, tend to be slower in adopting new technologies in their work. That is why, according to the SNA survey, 95% strongly agree with the idea of recruiting younger contract staff or volunteers to assist in technical works in SNA. And the fourth, and mostly related to the DM level, is the fact that a rather large percentage (around 20%, based on the SNA survey) have been assigned to tasks that are not suitable for their previous technical expertise. This issue is most pronounced at the DMK level, where officials transferred from line departments are put in charge of different sectors (Figure 14).

SNA officials have also been trained on gender and climate change. From the SNA survey, more than 60% of the respondents said they had attended trainings on gender 1–3 times, and about 20% for more than 3 times. However, on climate change, about 65% responded they had never attended a training on the topic (Figure 15).

At the national level, three factors have been identified. First, the incomplete legal framework, especially concerning the DMK functional transfer (discussed in the legal framework section above), has created confusion at the SNAs. While officials are aware of the functional transfer, for instance, they are either unaware or confused about what to do with them. Second, even without COVID-19 challenges, there has been limited

Figure 14: Key Perceptions and Awareness from the Subnational Administration Survey

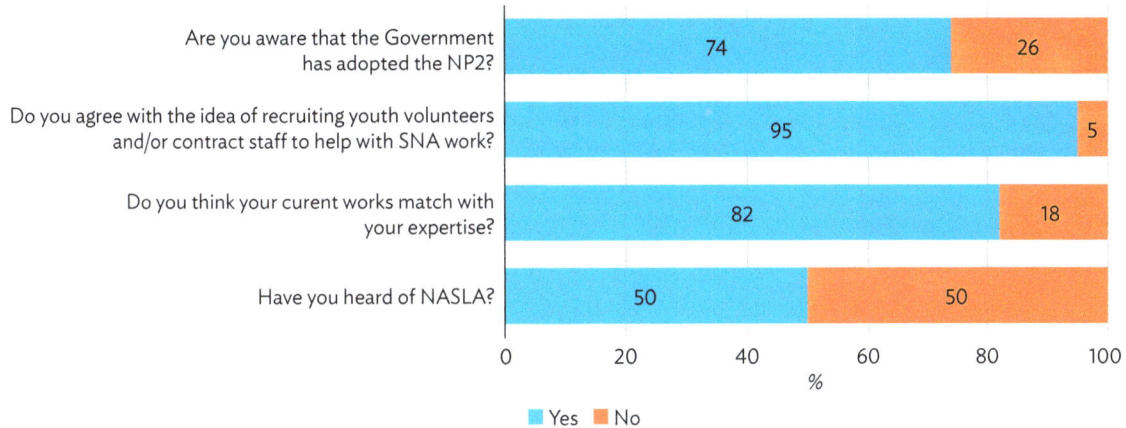

Are you aware that the Government has adopted the NP2?	74 / 26
Do you agree with the idea of recruiting youth volunteers and/or contract staff to help with SNA work?	95 / 5
Do you think your curent works match with your expertise?	82 / 18
Have you heard of NASLA?	50 / 50

(x-axis: 0, 20, 40, 60, 80, 100, %)

Legend: ■ Yes ■ No

NP2 = Second National Program on Sub-national Democratic Development, NASLA = National School for Local Administration, SNA = subnational administration.

Source: Authors' calculation based on the online surveys.

coordination among several actors providing training to SNAs. For instance, on budgeting matters, at least three agencies have been involved, including the general departments of MEF (including the General Department of Treasury), the Economic and Finance Institute, and NASLA. While effort has been made, coordination among the three still needs improvement. Third, based on perspectives from SNAs, capacity building through training alone would not be enough. Other complementary approaches suggested by SNA officials include the use of easy-to-understand online training videos, national-level help desks for SNAs, and mentoring of less experienced officials by the more experienced ones.

At the policy level, the SNA capacity issues need to be viewed in close connection to the question of functional transfer. This argument is particularly applicable to the DMK level. First, as of now, there are still no coherent and government-wide principles to guide the selection of functions to be transferred.[95] It also seems that capacity constraints were not given sufficient attention at the time of the functional transfer decision. This explains why, 3 years on, disagreement has started to emerge among key agencies (i.e., MEF, NCDD-S, and some line ministries) as to whether the 55 functions transferred in 2019 are appropriate for the DM level.[96] Second, capacity building at SNAs should be seen as a "learning by doing" approach, meaning SNAs will learn while taking on performing more functions given to them. In the current situation, as the functional transfer process slows or stalls, it would have direct implications on SNA capacity gains.

Figure 15: Trainings on Gender and Climate Change

Q: How many times have you attended the training on the following topics?

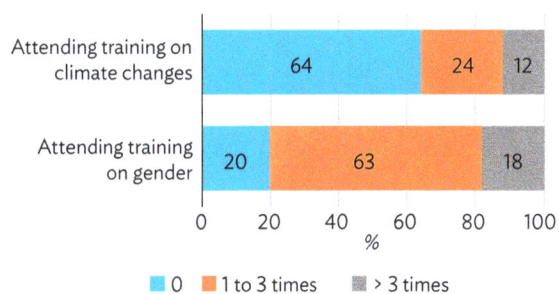

Attending training on climate changes	64 / 24 / 12
Attending training on gender	20 / 63 / 18

(x-axis: 0, 20, 40, 60, 80, 100, %)

Legend: ■ 0 ■ 1 to 3 times ▦ > 3 times

Source: Authors' calculation based on the online surveys.

---

95   (World Bank, 2022b).
96   MEF interview (20 May 2022), NCDD-S interview (18 May 2022).

Progress in SNDD reforms requires much more structured and systematic capacity development.
The capacity development under the 3-Year Implementation Plan Phase 1 (IP3-I) was supply-driven to a large extent by the need to provide learning around the legal framework, though it was more demand-driven in subsequent IP3. During IP3-II, provincial resource facilities were established to reduce the tendency of using long-term technical assistance for capacity substitution. Establishment of the NASLA was formalized under a sub-decree in 2016. As a national-level institution, NASLA aims to provide the platform for sustainable training that can be scaled up to develop a competent cadre of SNA staff capable of fulfilling their mandate for better subnational service delivery.

ASAC also has a role in SNA-building capacity especially of councilors. According to the Second NPSDD, ASAC is supposed to play two key roles in SNDD: first, as the voice of elected councilors and of councils as institutions in policy dialogue for SNDD; and second, as the provider of capacity development for elected councilors, who have different capacity development needs and require other skills sets from SNA officials. ASAC has its main office in Phnom Penh and presence in each province. From the surveys, however, the knowledge about ASAC at the provincial level is limited, both among SNA officials and NGOs who, in some cases, can work with ASAC to provide capacity building for SNA councilors (Figure 16).

The contribution of ASAC in promoting the roles of SNAs in CSDG has been highlighted through its recent work to produce the 2023 Voluntary Subnational Review for Cambodia. The review was conducted according to the UN VNR Handbook and United Cities and Local Government Guidelines. It examines the localization of SDGs within Cambodia by focusing on the CP and the DMK. It also conducted a survey with 172 randomly selected sample CP and DMK administrations.[97]

Figure 16: Knowledge About Association of Sub-National Administration Council

Q: Do you know about the existence of the ASAC in each province?

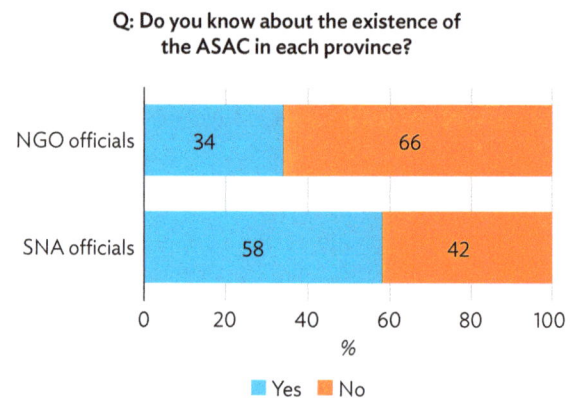

ASAC = Association of Sub-National Administration Council, NGO = nongovernment organization, SNA = subnational administration.

Source: Authors' calculation based on the online surveys.

E-government at Subnational Level

E-government and digitalization deserves more attention as it can help unleash much capacity at the SNA level. In the last few years, the government has adopted several policies to promote digitalization, including the Cambodia Digital Economy and Society Policy Framework 2021–2035, the Cambodia Digital Government Policy 2022–2035, and the Law on Electronic Commerce. It is learned from the interviews that the government is preparing an e-government strategy for SNAs. In drafting the policy, the interviews also revealed, there is a strong need to ensure that the e-government initiatives at the SNAs be aligned with the national e-government reform agenda. Equally important, the interviews indicate, the national e-government also needs to be in line with the decentralization reform, laws, and regulations.

---

[97]   (ASAC, 2023).

When discussing e-government, specific mechanisms are suggested to be given high priority. As suggested by the KIIs, those include the digitalization within the OWSU and OWSO where many administrative services such as licensing and document legalization have been provided; the expansion and improvement of the FMIS, which has become an essential tool for public financial management; and better sharing and use of the Commune Database (CDB), whose content might be helpful not just for government agencies but also NGOs working on local development and service delivery.

Digitalization was also mentioned as a key innovation to improve communication and capacity building for SNA officials. While many people were skeptical about SNA officials' ability to adopt digital technology in their works, the survey conducted for this study indicated that a large percentage of SNA officials have been using internet and social media for their works. More importantly, many of them have been experiencing online meeting (via Zoom) and regular use of Telegram for receiving updates on latest laws and policy documents. Interestingly, a relatively high percentage said they would be willing to continue using such a hybrid way of working and online platforms (as illustrated in Figure 17).

Figure 17: Experience and Perceptions of Subnational Administration Officials on Working with Digital Technology

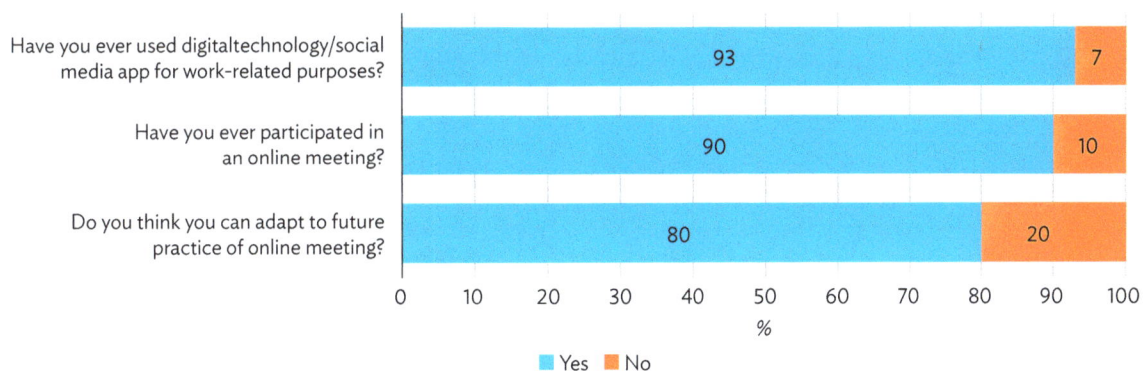

Source: Authors' calculation based on the online surveys.

Budgeting, Functional Assignment, and Planning at Subnational Administrations

Appropriate functional assignment, followed by resource transfer, is essential to SNAs' ability to contribute to the achievement of SDGs. In the international literature and Cambodia's policy, critical aspects are given attention, including expenditure and revenue assignment, functional assignment, planning, and the public financial management (PFM) process at the SNAs. This section will refer to existing literature and policy documents for the details about budget allocation, planning, and PFM at SNAs while highlighting key findings to which the government should pay more attention.

In this report, a few key points are noted. First, as far as contributing to the SDG achievement is concerned, SNAs have been given bigger budgets in the last decade. However, vertical and horizontal imbalances remain a key challenge, together with limited own-source revenue. Second, the functional assignment process needs urgent attention for both policy and implementation, especially at the DMK level, where many functions expected to be transferred can have direct impact on the CSDGs. Finally, SNA planning needs further streamlining with data so that resources and efforts can be better aligned with the national development priority and thus the CSDGs.

Expenditure and Revenue Share and Trends

Existing data show upward trends in budget allocation to SNAs, both in absolute and relative terms. SNA total expenditure as the shared of total national expenditure increased from just below 7% in 2018 to almost 13% in 2023. If external financing is excluded from the total national expenditure, the SNA share went from 8.5% in 2018 to over 15% in 2023. Compared to other countries, especially those in the region, the share is still low, but it has shown noticeable progress compared to the period from 2015 to 2018 (Figures 18 and 19).

Figure 18: Subnational Administration Expenditure as Percentage of Total National Expenditure, 2018–2023

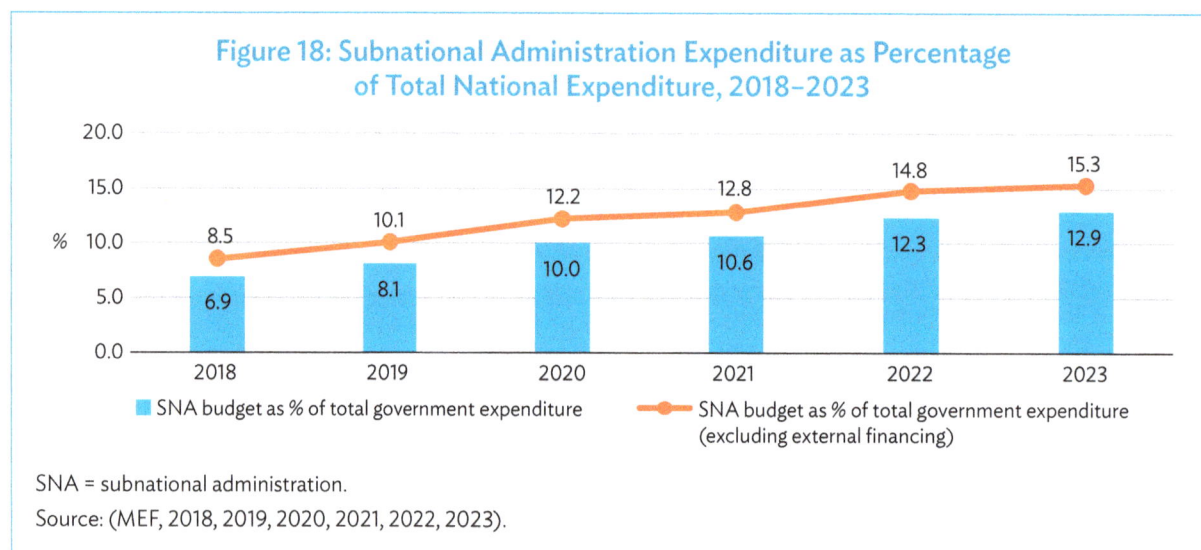

SNA = subnational administration.
Source: (MEF, 2018, 2019, 2020, 2021, 2022, 2023).

Figure 19: Share of Subnational Administration Expenditure in Total National Expenditure, 2015–2018

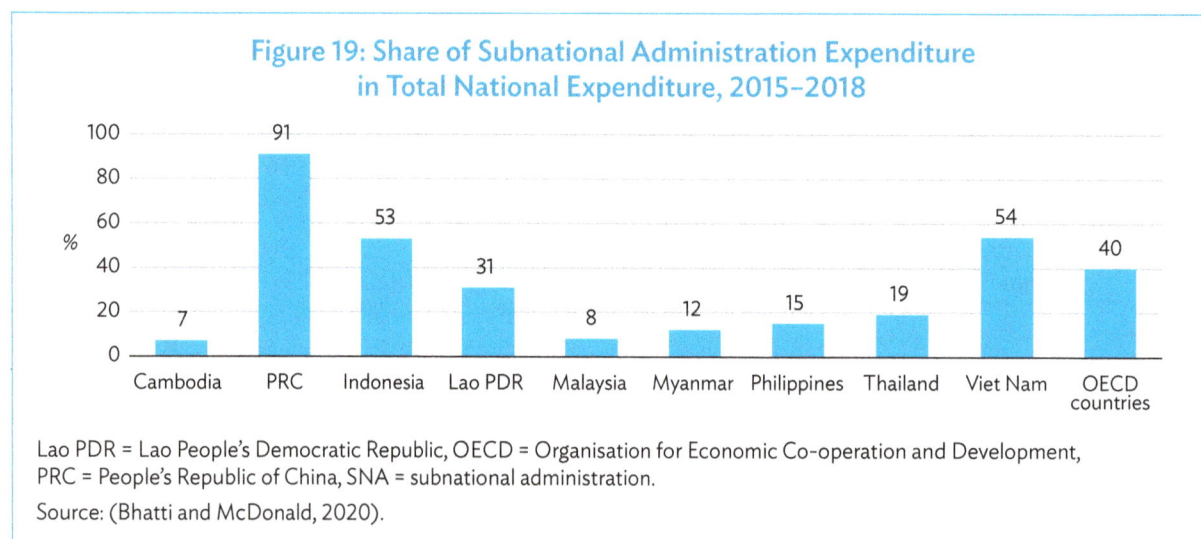

Lao PDR = Lao People's Democratic Republic, OECD = Organisation for Economic Co-operation and Development, PRC = People's Republic of China, SNA = subnational administration.
Source: (Bhatti and McDonald, 2020).

Despite the improvement, both vertical and horizontal imbalances have been the main challenge in the way budget is allocated to SNAs in Cambodia. Vertically, the CP level has taken almost 70% of the total SNA budget, while the DMK level, despite being the expected main tier for service delivery, accounts for only 13%. Horizontally, between 2011 and 2021, on average, Phnom Penh's annual budget accounted for about 55% of total SNA budget. In 2011, it stood at about 45% and from there steadily increased to almost 60% in 2020 but dropped back to slightly above 50% (Figures 20 and 21).

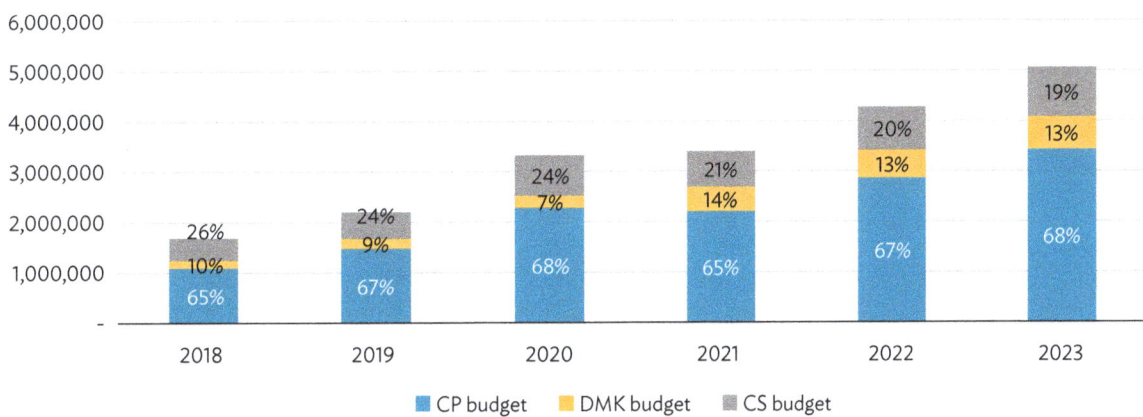

Figure 20: Subnational Administration Expenditure by Tiers, 2018–2023
(in KR million)

CP = Capital and Provincial; CS = Commune and Sangkat; DMK = District, Municipality, and Khan; SNA = subnational administration.
Source: RGC (2018, 2019, 2020, 2021, 2022, 2023).

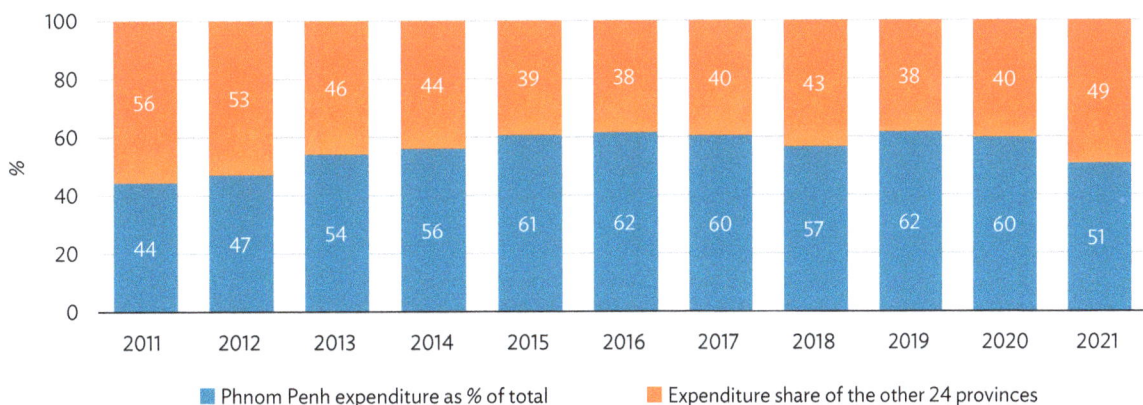

Figure 21: Phnom Penh Budget as Percentage of Total Subnational Administration Budget

Source: Authors' calculation based on data provided by MEF (2022).

The limited use of the Classification of the Functions of Government makes it hard to link SNA expenditure with specific CSDGs. Although the classification has been adopted by the government, its actual record has been uneven. Available data suggest that much of the development spending by SNAs fall under "transportation" (Code 7045) and a few on "water supply" (Code 7063).[98] Under the PFM reform, according to the interview, the government, especially MEF, has been pushing for more systematic use of the classification in the reporting of SNA budget.

Revenue assignment has been limited, although some progress has been made on the nontax revenue side. The ability of SNAs to collect own-source revenue implies their higher autonomy and flexibility to use their budget to meet local needs. It also implies stronger accountability from SNAs to their own citizens. In Cambodia, available data show that, for SNAs altogether, their own resource accounted for about 65% in 2018 but only 48% in 2023. The disaggregated data further suggest that most of the own source revenue has been collected mainly by the CP level, and virtually none for the DMK and CS level (Figure 22).

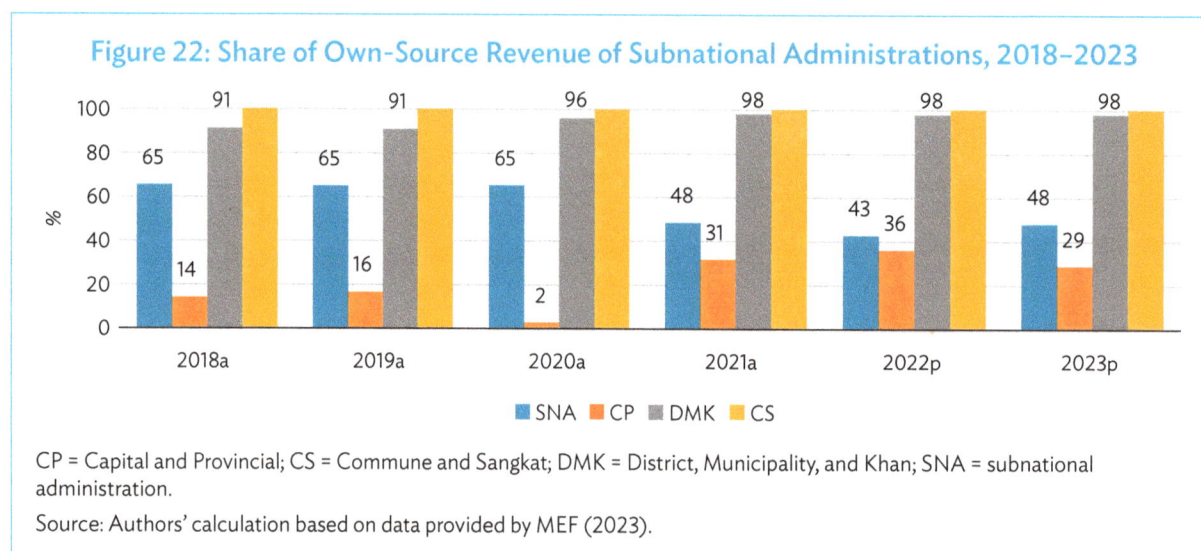

Figure 22: Share of Own-Source Revenue of Subnational Administrations, 2018–2023

CP = Capital and Provincial; CS = Commune and Sangkat; DMK = District, Municipality, and Khan; SNA = subnational administration.

Source: Authors' calculation based on data provided by MEF (2023).

The government has plans to transfer more nontax revenue but not tax revenue items to the SNA. The Law on Non-Tax Revenue and the KIIs indicate that SNAs will have more authority and roles in collecting more nontax revenue in the form of fees of public services (especially those provided through the OWSU and OWSO) and state assets. More regulations and implementation arrangements, however, are needed for SNAs to be able to plan, collect, and manage the revenue related to state assets.[99]

Functional Assignment

Functional assignment, while critical in any decentralization reform, has progressed only slowly and unevenly in Cambodia. International practices suggest that clear and rationale assignment of functions is critical to allow SNAs to contribute to the achievement of national priorities and, by extension, CSDGs. In Cambodia,

---

[98]   For more information about Classification of the Functions of Government, please see (IMF, 2001).
[99]   For more information, please see (World Bank, 2022c).

as documented in recent literature, the functional assignment has progressed slowly, with many challenges lying ahead.[100] This report wishes to highlight a few key points that the government should concentrate on.

Since 2009, uneven progress has been made on the functional transfers. One exception is the delegation of functions from line ministries to the CP OWSU and DMK OWSO. In 2019, the progress was accelerated when 55 sector functions were transferred to the DMK in one go. After 3 years, all key stakeholders agree that the transfer has not been complete, and that the implementation of the transferred functions is still very much in doubt. As discussed above, key agencies have come up with concrete plans on how to address these challenges, but equally important (if not more) is how committed the line ministries are to the reform process. From the interviews conducted for this assignment, line ministries have given much attention to the decentralization reform, especially after the 2019 transfer. However, their progress and challenges differ.

More progress is noted for social sectors, especially those with long experience with decentralization and deconcentration. The main example was the full transfer of functions performed by the Provincial Health Department from the Ministry of Health to the CP administration. The education sector has been more reluctant, limiting the full transfer (similar to the case of the Ministry of Health) to only one province, Battambang. The Ministry of Social Affairs, Veterans, and Youth made noticeable progress in managing the state orphanages since the function was transferred in 2017. The first 2 years reportedly faced some issues with unclear instructions and delays in the budget execution process that had to go through the provincial administration as the new budget manager. But the problem was reportedly addressed starting from the 2020 fiscal year.

Less progress has been noticeable for economic sector ministries, although much effort has been made. As a starting point, economic sector ministries such as agriculture, irrigation management, clean water supply, and rural development are much less deconcentrated in terms of budget compared to those in the social sector. For these ministries, except for the functions transferred to OWSU and OWSO (mentioned above), little progress has been made since the 2019 reform. However, from the interviews, much effort is going on. For instance, Ministry of Agriculture, Forestry, and Fisheries expects to have the new guideline for the DMK on how to perform the newly transferred functions to be approved by its minister soon. Ministry of Environment has been working to further monitor and improve the way the DM implement the transferred functions on solid waste management.[101]

In the next few years, the more pressing challenge is the functional assignment to the DMK level. As mentioned above, the government has already adopted sub-decrees transferring 55 functions to this tier. However, the implementation has been limited. First, at the policy level, there have not been decisions to classify the 55 functions (and their sub-functions) into obligatory versus permissive functions and to stipulate the relevant funding mechanisms for each. Second, no costing had been done to identify the amount of budget needed to perform the transferred functions. Without such information, the budget discussion has referred mainly to the previous budget allocations that line ministries and their provincial departments had used to perform the functions before the transfer.

Personnel shortage and the limited understanding at DMK about the transfer are other main challenges. On personnel, except for the Ministry of Interior (MOI) and Ministry of Education, Youth, and Sport (MEYS), other ministries such as tourism, mining, commerce, and labor have transferred only small number of staff members to the DMK. As with the understanding of the DMK administration themselves, according to the fieldwork, while many are aware about the transfers, they often lack knowledge on what this means for their works and responsibilities. Please see Box 3 for more information about recent progress in personnel transfer to SNAs.

---

[100] For more information, please see (World Bank, 2022b).
[101] Based on SNA interviews, interview with NCDD, and interviews with MAFF D&D working group.

Box 3: Latest Progress and Challenges in Personnel Transfer to Subnational Administrations

Despite some progress, personnel transfer and deployment to subnational administrations (SNAs) remain challenging. Following the 2013 Policy on the Management and Development of Human Resource at SNAs and various legal documents, there has been an increase in staff transfers to SNAs. However, sector-specific deployment still poses problems. For example, as of January 2020, nearly 20,000 staff members were transferred to the district, municipality, and khan (DMK) administration, predominantly from the Ministry of Interior and the Ministry of Education, Youth, and Sport. In contrast, other ministries such as tourism, mining, commerce, and labor transferred fewer than 50 staff members across the country, which has over 200 DMKs. The number of personnel transferred tends to correlate more with the number of DMK rather than economic activities. For instance, Sihanoukville, despite its economic importance, received only 137 civil servants from line ministries, a figure similar to or lower than provinces like Steung Treng, Kratie, Udor Meanchey, and Koh Kong.[a]

There are reasons for cautious optimism in addressing personnel shortages at the subnational level. For example, following the transfer of functions in the education sector, prompt action was taken to transfer pre-school, nonformal, and primary education staff to the DMK administrations. Similarly, the Ministry of Agriculture, Forestry, and Fisheries, traditionally slow in decentralization reform, has made significant strides by recruiting about 1,600 agricultural technical staff to be stationed in nearly every commune/sangkat. These staff are tasked with conducting farmers' needs assessments, reporting to line agencies, coordinating solutions, facilitating links within agricultural value chains, and collecting and transmitting agricultural statistics.[b]

Despite these initiatives, several challenges remain. Firstly, the government must ensure that new working arrangements and accountability lines between these technical staff, DMK councils, and line ministries are clearly established and understood. Secondly, it needs to ensure adequate non-wage budget allocation to support the activities of transferred and newly recruited staff. For instance, the draft 2024 budget allocates $4 million to support the newly recruited 1,600 agricultural technical staff, a sum that is barely sufficient to cover wages, leaving limited funds for non-wage operational costs.

[a]   Based on the budget data provided by the NCDD-S team, 2021.
[b]   Please see https://www.youtube.com/watch?v=p5rD6ByM90s&list=PLHLaLvqMR3wZaGNZIN8hFBK-fjEeCX7jN&index=4.
Sources: (RGC, 2023f) (RGC, 2013) (MEYS, 2023).

The second point that this report wishes to highlight is the limited provision on the regulatory roles of SNAs. There seems to be an expectation among local-level officials and certain advocacy groups that the SNAs need to have much more budget from the national level to actually provide the services assigned to them. This expectation partly reflects an assumption that the SNAs will actually provide those services themselves. However, from the fieldwork, for some key basic services such as clean water and solid waste management, SNAs do not necessarily need to provide the services themselves, but can also play coordinating, regulating, and supporting roles in partnership with the private sectors to ensure the services are delivered. The section on partnerships will discuss more about the private sector engagement at the local level in Cambodia.

The third point is the distinction between urban and rural areas when it comes to functional transfer. It should be noted the 2019 sub-decrees on the transfer of functions to the DMK level did entail distinctions about urban SNAs (here being the municipality and khan) and rural SNAs (here being the district).[102] However, given the fast-paced urbanization that Cambodia has experienced during the last 2 decades, more detailed policy provisions, technical guidelines, and statistics are needed to identify the appropriate functions and tasks that urban SNAs should perform as opposed to their rural peers.

---

[102]   For more information, please see (RGC, 2019b).

The legal framework around the obligatory versus permissive functions needs to be clarified. Laws and regulations give powers, roles, and responsibilities to SNAs to provide public services and local development through the performance of their obligatory and optional functions under their jurisdiction. However, the many functions transferred to SNAs have not been clearly defined as obligatory or optional. This legal gap has been well acknowledged in the Second NPSDD. What this study found in the addition is that, with the unclear functional definition, SNAs tend to allocate more of their budget to local infrastructure projects (especially roads) and much less on social services. By extension, this also implies less contribution from SNAs on SDGs focusing on social as opposed to economic development.

Concerning the DMK level, more attention is needed on the consistencies between sector rules and regulations and the Sub-decrees Nos. 182, 183, and 184. As mentioned, the sub-decrees transfer many functions from line ministries to the DMK administrations. The transfer also implies changes to the ways some functions are to be performed. For instance, it would be the DMK administrations and not line departments who should implement the service delivery. In addition, certain aspects of the planning process, licensing process, M&E, and reporting lines were expected to change. However, KIIs suggest that, even as of 2022, some line ministries, through their provincial line departments, continued to implement the transferred functions and rely on their existing rules and procedures. This has not only slowed down the functional transferred process but created confusion among the DMK officials expected to perform the newly transferred functions.

Subnational Planning

In line with the current legal and policy framework, SNAs prepare and adopt 5-year Development Plans and 3-year Investment Plans. The Board of Governors (BOG) prepares and submits the two plans to the council for adoption, following relevant provisions of the Organic Law and regulations on subnational planning.[103] An interministerial Prakas #0149 was adopted in 2020 to revise the timeline in the preparation of the 3-year Investment Plan so that it is aligned with that of the provincial Budget Strategic Plan (BSP). However, because the reform is still new, some SNAs still have not followed the new time frame. The MOP, MOI, and MEF have also been monitoring and supporting the implementation of this new guideline.[104]

SNA 5-year Development Plans and 3-year Investment Plans need to be aligned with the NSDP and by extension to the SDGs. On this point, the government, especially MEF, has made significant progress in the last 3 years. As guided by the SNA Budget System Reform Strategy (SNA-BSRS), each CP has developed a BSP that integrates all the investment plans of all SNAs and aligns all the plans of line departments toward achieving specific development objectives in the four sectors. SNA plans are also expected to be better linked to the NSDP (and, by extension, the SDGs) through the implementation of the program-based budgeting. This has only been introduced to the CP level. For this level, their budget must be formulated along four programs, divided into various subprograms, and activity clusters, as presented below. The program budgeting at the SNA level, however, has just started.

For SNA planning purposes, much data have been collected on local needs but very limited data have been collected in regard to line ministries' interventions, donor projects, NGOs, and private financing. In preparing the annual 3-year Investment Plan, the current guidelines[105] expect the production and use of a wide range of data. However, based on the KIIs, not much information is available on major projects managed by line departments and line ministries, including those funded by development partners. This implies that a substantial part of development interventions in SNAs are not included into the 3-year Investment Plan, given that most line ministry projects tend to be large in scope. Data are also limited when it comes to investment and financing

---

[103] (World Bank, 2022b).
[104] MOP interview (20 April 2022).
[105] (MOI and MOP, 2020).

by NGOs and the private sector. This lack of data reflects the current situation where central ministries still hold much authority over investment approval and licensing, as well as the over the operation of NGOs. When it comes to interacting with these non-state actors, the provincial administration is mainly limited to a coordinating role, which is yet to be clarified.

Spatial planning has also been prepared in big urban areas, although some challenges remain. With the Provincial Department of Land Management taking the lead, capital and some provincial, DMK, and CS administrations have managed to prepare their land-use planning. However, many SNAs have not taken the steps. This is partly because of capacity and resource constraints in those localities. Another challenge is that SNAs need to have a better understanding of how to link their socioeconomic planning (i.e., the 5-year Development Plans and 3-year Investment Plans) more explicitly and systematically with their land-use planning.

The lack of uniformity in defining and aligning various sectors and subsectors in national and SNA planning and budgeting is a key issue connecting SNA plans to CSDG. As Table 6 demonstrates, there are differing classifications of sectors and/or indicators across the CSDGs, the NSDP, and the planning and budgeting processes for SNAs. For the VNR, efforts were made to harmonize the indicators of the CSDGs and NSDP. However, similar alignment has not been pursued for SNAs. More critically, inconsistencies are also evident at the aggregate level in sector classification for SNA planning, as directed by the NCDD, and SNA budgeting, as guided by the MEF. This inconsistency is expected to be more pronounced at more detailed levels (such as subsectors, subprograms, activity clusters) and in the classification of indicators (for instance, NSDP at the national level and CDB for SNAs).

Table 6: Classification of Sectors or Indicators at National and Subnational Levels

Key Policies/Tools	Classification of Sectors or Indicators
CSDG	SDG 1 through SDG 18
NSDP	• Agriculture, forestry, and fisheries • Rural development • Transport • Health • Education • De-mining
Line ministries (relevant to functional transfers to SNAs)	• Land Management, Urban Planning, Construction • Rural Development • Water Resources and Meteorology • Environment • Mines and Energy • Agriculture, Forestry, and Fishery • Public Works and Transport • Industry and Handicraft • Commerce • Tourism • Social Affairs, Veterans, and Youth Rehabilitation • Women Affairs • Labor and Vocational Training • Cults and Religion • Culture and Fine Arts • Posts and Telecommunications • Health • Education, Youth, and Sports

continued on next page

Table 6 *continued*

Key Policies/Tools	Classification of Sectors or Indicators
SNA Planning	• Economic development, • Social development • Natural resources, environment, and climate change adaptation • General administration, security, and public orders
SNA Budgeting	• Economic development • Social development • Security & public orders • General administration

CSDG = Cambodian Sustainable Development Goal, NSPD = National Strategic Development Plan, SDG = Sustainable Development Goal, SNA = subnational administration.

Source: Prepared by the authors.

Accountability Mechanisms, Monitoring and Evaluation, and Data Work

This section explores how data collection and monitoring efforts consider subnational efforts and which local SDG data and monitoring initiatives exist, e.g., local M&E frameworks, local data collection, or voluntary local and subnational reviews.

As Cambodia is a unitary state, SNAs are considered part of the government's broader check-and-balance system but with their own specific autonomy. From their development plans to budgets to personnel, SNAs are supposed to operate within a national legal and policy framework. For instance, development plans need to be aligned with national development priorities, and budgets are formulated, approved, and monitored as a part of the overall macroeconomic framework, along with medium-term and annual budget processes. However, SNAs are also given specific autonomy to ensure that they can truly represent and respond to the needs of their local citizens. These include, among other things, the autonomy in development planning process, budget allocation, human resources management, etc.

Democratic accountability mechanisms have been built into the structure of the SNAs. At the three tiers of SNAs, a council is elected to represent the people in their locality and to check and hold the executive part of the administration accountable. The assessment so far has been that, for the CS administration where the councils are directly elected by the people, they have played active roles in deciding and monitoring the development activities, including planning and budgeting.[106] According to the KIIs at SNA level, for DMK and CP administrations, where the councils are indirectly elected, i.e., by elected CS councilors and not by local citizens, the representative power of the council in holding the BOG accountable has been weaker. The government well recognizes this limitation and has stipulated specific policy actions as stated in the Second NPSDD.[107]

At the subnational level, while mechanisms of political representation still exist, no real political competition is observed. SNA councils at all levels are supposed to represent people from different competing political parties. The councils continue to play their mandates, but with the only main opposition party dissolved back in 2017, no real political competition can be seen at the subnational level. When there is only one political party

---

[106] (World Bank and TAF, 2013).
[107] (NCDD, 2021).

in the driving seat, the availability of balancing voices from civil societies and private sectors has become even more necessary.

SNA governance system also has built-in mechanisms for civic engagement. Those mechanisms are listed in the Technical Guideline on Civic Engagement (2014). The most important is people's participation in the local planning process. In this annual event, villagers are gathered to raise their needs which are then compiled and prioritized so that they can be funded either by state budget or NGO budgets. The participation, according to the SNA interviews and survey, has been decreasing in the last 5 years, however. The trend, as it was explained, was due to several factors, including the out-migration of young people; COVID-19 restraints on people gathering; and most importantly, a sense of participation fatigue given the limited capacity of the SNAs to respond.

Besides the built-in democratic check-and-balance structure, other accountability mechanisms have been developed and improved over time. Those include the administrative and reporting requirement that SNAs must comply with regarding their functioning, ranging from planning, budgeting, and human resources management. Another important accountability is the establishment of CP and DMK ombudsman offices throughout the country. The ombudsman offices offer a quick and free public grievance redress mechanism, allowing for citizens to file complaints on maladministration in the functioning of the SNAs.[108] Both SNAs and national KIIs suggest, however, that there has been less engagement from local people in using these grievance mechanisms and that more needs to be understood as to why. CSOs have played essential roles in holding SNAs accountable.

Bottom–up communication and feedback from the subnational level to the national level require urgent attention. As a long-term strategy, the Second NPSDD also seeks to develop and implement a communication strategy to promote awareness and exchange of information among key stakeholders of the reform, including between national and subnational levels. While all these measures are applauded, one important gap requires urgent attention: the bottom–up feedback loop from the subnational level to the policymakers at the national level. So far, as the functional transfer continues, the feedback loop has been uneven at best. As such, it is not known (at least, not in a timely manner) what has and has not worked, and what adjustments are needed in the policy.

Internal audit functions at SNAs have yet to be developed. The reform on auditing in the public sector in Cambodia is still at an early stage. At the national level, internal audit was introduced in 2006 in order to accompany the decentralization of financial management to line ministries. As of the end of 2016, almost all line ministries had internal audit units. However, the overall legal framework for internal audit and inspection still needs further clarification. In 2020, the government adopted Sub-decree No. 168 to clarify the functions and duties of internal audits on top of the various legal and procedural documents before it. However, for SNAs, many details are yet to be put in place, for instance, with regard to the procedures and steps of the internal audits.

In the context of decentralization, specific progress has been made in recent years. In late 2019, as a part of the restructuring of the DMK administrations, the government created the Internal Control Office under the Administration Director. Since then, however, precise terms of reference and working procedures for this office have not been formulated. At the CP level, a similar office has not been created. There is also a need to clarify the roles of the MOI in performing external audits over SNAs, in general. At the NCDD-S, an internal audit has also been established to conduct audits but mainly for donor-funded projects implemented under NCDD-S. The mandate of this internal audit unit over SNAs has not been clearly defined. In 2019, the NCDD adopted the

---

[108] ADB has also supported ombudsman offices through its policy dialogue to strengthen its functioning and integrate gender considerations.

guideline for internal audit. But the document is said to be too complicated and unclear as to how far it can be applied to SNA internal audit.

External audit is conducted by the National Audit Authority (NAA). Established since 2001, NAA is the supreme audit institution of Cambodia, and a member of the International Organization Supreme Audit Institutions. The auditor-general and deputy auditor-general are appointed by royal decree on the recommendation of Cambodia and approved by majority plus one of all members of the national assembly. NAA performs the external audit of Cambodia, and reports to the National Assembly, Senate, and the government, aiming at promoting good governance and improving the efficiency of the public sector, as well as contributing to the successful implementation of strategies, policies, and reform programs. The Audit Law provides the NAA with the mandate to conduct an audit on the public sector agencies, including SNAs.[109] The law only mentions SNAs but offers no other specific provisions on the external audit to be conducted at these levels. The NAA is expected to send the audit reports to the Parliament, Senate, and to the Royal Government of Cambodia for information.

In practice, external audits on SNAs have been rare for CP administrations and never been done for DMK and CS. Among those rare exercises, one example was the external audit done on the Phnom Penh Capital Administration back in 2015. While the audit report was supposed to be publicly available, in reality, the report has not been widely shared even within the government, including key ministries such as the MEF and MOI. In some cases, actions recommended by the NAA were followed up and acted upon, but there has not been much dissemination and discussion on those. In the case of the Phnom Penh Capital Administration, for instance, it was reported that the NAA submits the audit on budget settlement law to the legislature within 3 months after receiving the draft of budget settlement law for the last three completed years. However, it was not sure what was done with the submitted report.

Cambodia conducted the VNR back in 2019 and more recently in late 2022. From the KIIs, the 2019 VNR was largely a national government exercise, led by the MOP, and with participation of the MOI and ASAC representing the SNAs. It was indicated that the data used for the VNR were largely based on the national level, while SNA data (such as the CDB, SNA administrative reports, etc.) were not used.

For planning and reporting purposes, SNAs are required to collect a substantial amount of data. Those datasets are listed in Table 7. Such data have been used mostly for planning and routine reporting purposes. Those include monthly reports that SNAs have to prepare for the BOG and the council. So, the reports focus mainly on budget execution and inputs/activities performed. According to the SNA-BSRS, the impact evaluation system for SNAs is yet to be developed until after 2025. In the meantime, the focus is on ensuring regular and systematic monitoring, especially on outputs and budget.

Limited effectiveness in data storage, sharing, and use has increasingly become a key challenge to the current SNA reporting exercise. For the provincial level, the workload of collecting and storing falls on the Provincial Development Plan and the Planning and Investment Unit of the provincial administration. The PDP, as the permanent member of the Planning Working Group, possesses and stores much of the data, but it also needs to get data from line departments and SNAs. According to the KIIs, such data sharing and data storage has not been smooth nor systematic. Most of the data are kept in Microsoft Word or Excel format on various computers, vulnerable to data loss, authorized changes, or clerical errors. At the DMK level, the data management falls under the Planning and Investment Unit, while at the CS level, it is the responsibility of the clerks.

---

[109] (RGC, 2000), Article 2.

**Table 7: Key Datasets Expected to Be Used in Subnational Administration
3-Year Investment Plan Preparation**

SNA	Types of data
CS level	• CS 5-year Development Plan and related tables • CS 3-year Investment Plan without available funding • Subnational project development plans from previous years • Tables on problems, needs, and solutions from previous years • Socioeconomic situation report (prepared by Provincial Dept of Planning) • CS scorecard (prepared by Provincial Dept of Planning) • CS administrative map and social service mapping (if any) • Cambodian Sustainable Development Goals • Financing sources of NGOs and other actors • CP and DMK 5-year Development Plan (as broader references)
DMK level	• Relevant information/data provided by the CS administrations • DMK 5-year Development Plan and related tables • DMK 3-year Investment Plan without available funding • Subnational project development plans from previous years • Tables on problems, needs, and solutions from previous years • Financing sources of NGOs and other actors • Need analysis by sectors and subsectors (as prepared by technical offices under the DMK administrations)
CP level	• Relevant information/data provided by the CS and DMK • CP 5-year Development Plan and related tables • CP 3-year Investment Plan without available funding • BSP of sector line department • Financing sources of NGOs and other actors

BSP = budget strategic plan; CP = Capital and Provincial; CS = Commune and Sangkat; DMK = District, Municipality, and Khan; NGO = nongovernment organization; SNA = subnational administration.
Source: (MOI and MOP, 2020).

The rollout of FMIS, although still new and limited to the CP level, is expected to improve reporting and data management at the SNA level. According to the reform plan, CP administrations will be ready to adopt the FMIS from 2022 onward. Up to 2020, it was the Provincial Department of Economy and Finance (PDEF), which helped enter financial information to FMIS for the administration. In 2022, per MEF's instruction No. 002, the FMIS was rolled out to all CP administrations, covering four main functions: budget allocation, purchases, accounts payment, and accounts receivable. For the DMK and CS level, in 2022, an FMIS Portal was also rolled out in 2022 but focused only on selected districts and communes.[110]

Multi–stakeholder Engagements and Partnerships, and Knowledge Solutions

Local participation, together with engagement and partnership with key stakeholders, is critical for ensuring better local service delivery and democratic development. As mentioned earlier, these principles are well stipulated in the existing policy on decentralization reforms in Cambodia. This study finds that such engagement has been positively assessed by key informants and survey respondents, although it has been uneven and more

---

[110]   (MEF, 2022b) (MEF, 2022c).

needs to be done. One area that requires new ways of thinking and new level of commitment is on knowledge solutions which are linked to data management and sharing.

Engagement with Civil Society Organizations

Existing policy and legal frameworks expect SNAs to collaborate with the private sector in service delivery. According to the Second NPSDD (Component 5), the collaboration with the private sector can take the following forms:

- A company/CSO with a contract from the SNA to deliver services, funded from the budget of the SNA.
- A company or CSO providing fee-based services under an agreement with the SNA (the benefits are financed from the fees revenue, not from the SNA budget).
- A public–private partnership in which the SNA is the owner of assets used by a firm to deliver services; for example, a waste disposal site is owned by the SNA but operated by a private firm.

Surveyed NGOs claimed to have made various contributions to local governance and development, but they have not received much information from the government. As Figure 23 shows, a high percentage of surveyed NGO officials said their organizations have provided services to local citizens (68%) and brought voices from local people to SNA officials (61%). However, fewer of them (42%) reported having heard that Cambodia adopted the Second NPSDD (back in mid-2022), received information about the budget of the SNAs in the areas where they work (22%), joined in the district integration workshop (42%), and joined in the policy consultation on decentralization with the government (34%).

Figure 23: Experiences of Surveyed Nongovernment Organizations on Key Engagement Questions

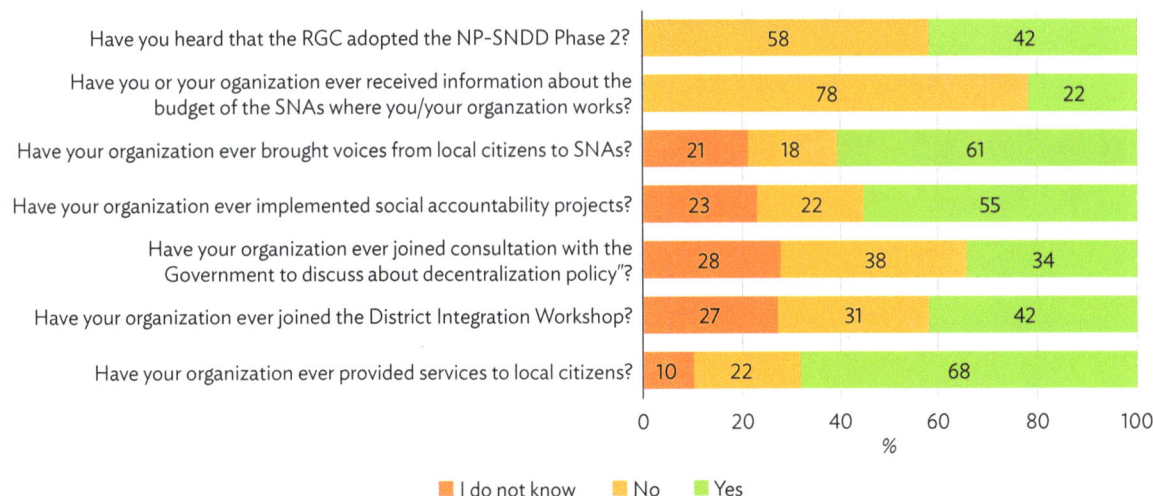

Question	I do not know	No	Yes
Have you heard that the RGC adopted the NP-SNDD Phase 2?		58	42
Have you or your oganization ever received information about the budget of the SNAs where you/your organzation works?		78	22
Have your organization ever brought voices from local citizens to SNAs?	21	18	61
Have your organization ever implemented social accountability projects?	23	22	55
Have your organization ever joined consultation with the Government to discuss about decentralization policy"?	28	38	34
Have your organization ever joined the District Integration Workshop?	27	31	42
Have your organization ever provided services to local citizens?	10	22	68

NP-SNDD = National Program on Sub-National Democratic Development, RGC = Royal Government of Cambodia, SNA = subnational administration.

Source: Authors' calculation based on the online surveys.

The Implementation of Social Accountability Framework (ISAF) is one channel through which local NGOs can work with SNAs. ISAF is an initiative seeking to improve local service delivery by focusing on the demand side. It aims to empower citizens and strengthen partnerships between SNAs and citizens. ISAF was introduced as a platform for coordinated action by the government and civil society to operationalize the Strategic Plan on Social Accountability for Sub-National Democratic Development adopted in 2013. In Phase 1, ISAF focused mainly on the CS level. In Phase 2, the initiative was expanded to DM level, with a focus on four areas: i) access to information and open budgets; ii) citizen monitoring; iii) capacity building and facilitation; and iv) program management, learning, and monitoring. From the NGO survey, about 55% of them said they had implemented the ISAF projects.

Despite the unevenness and some constraints, the surveyed NGO officials provided a fairly positive picture in terms of their collaboration with government. First, they indicated that they work together on various issues, but more noticeably in the areas of social service delivery, gender, and social protection. Second, as shown in Figure 24, more than 50% said their working relationship was better compared to 5 years ago, while less than 15% said it got worse. The relationship, it is learned from KIIs, tends to be more challenging for NGOs working on politically sensitive topics such as human rights, land, and national resource protection. Third, as shown in Figure 25, it is noted that CS level is still the main target for most NGOs working at the local level. The DMKs, where many service delivery functions will lie, reportedly have the least interaction with NGOs. This is one area for improvement, especially in the context of the functional transfer to the DMK administration.

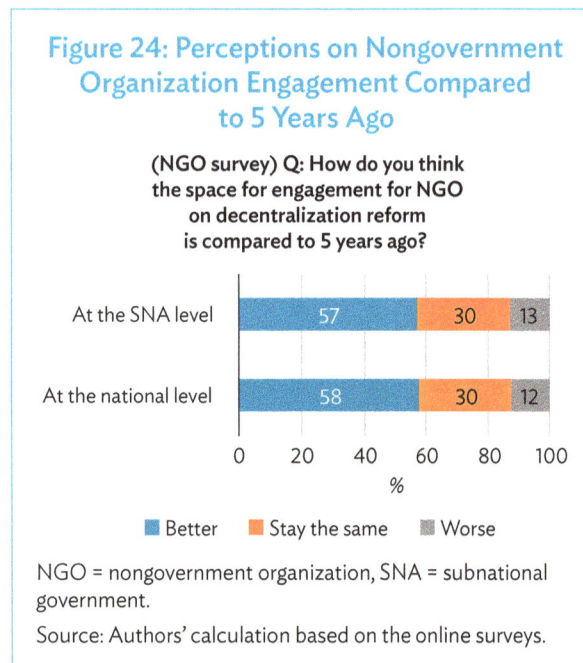

Figure 24: Perceptions on Nongovernment Organization Engagement Compared to 5 Years Ago

(NGO survey) Q: How do you think the space for engagement for NGO on decentralization reform is compared to 5 years ago?

At the SNA level: 57 | 30 | 13

At the national level: 58 | 30 | 12

■ Better   ■ Stay the same   ■ Worse

NGO = nongovernment organization, SNA = subnational government.

Source: Authors' calculation based on the online surveys.

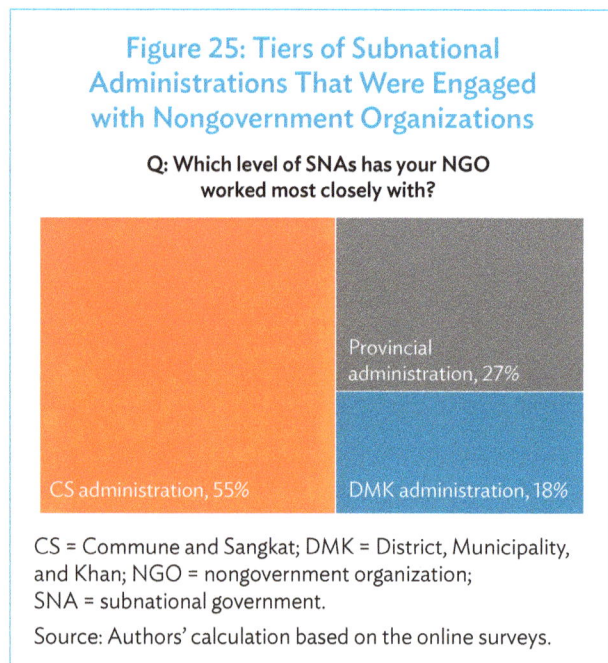

Figure 25: Tiers of Subnational Administrations That Were Engaged with Nongovernment Organizations

Q: Which level of SNAs has your NGO worked most closely with?

Provincial administration, 27%

CS administration, 55%

DMK administration, 18%

CS = Commune and Sangkat; DMK = District, Municipality, and Khan; NGO = nongovernment organization; SNA = subnational government.

Source: Authors' calculation based on the online surveys.

Engagement with the Private Sector

The Second NPSDD expects the partnership with the private sector to be delivered through several actions. These include 1) registration of local businesses or enterprises; 2) developing and implementing appropriate models of partnership with the private sector (including public–private partnerships); and 3) developing and implementing a framework for contracting-out of public services. Specific actions are proposed for each of the main actions, but more needs to be learned, especially when developing the mentioned models and frameworks.

The engagement of the private sector with the DMKs deserves more attention given the administration's expected roles in service delivery. DMKs are expected to work with the private sector in a systematic and regular ways. At the DM level, according to Sub-decrees Nos. 182 and 184, the engagement is expected to happen through the existing participatory planning process and/or specific mechanisms and instructions created by specific DMK administrations. The sub-decrees also mention that DMK administrations need to hold regular meetings with the private sector and CSOs to identify and solve the problems of local people. In reality, the inclusion of non-state actor financing and investment in the local plans has been minimal and uneven.

The private sector has been the main driver of growth and local service delivery in both social and economic sectors. KIIs confirmed that, especially in urban and fast-urbanizing areas, the private sector has been actively providing services in education (especially for secondary and university-level education), health, piped water, and waste management. In the economic sector, private businesses have also been behind the operation of some successful irrigation schemes, provision of agricultural inputs, and the operation of various types of eco-tourism resorts.

Despite the significance of contribution, data on private sector investments and financing in various sectors at SNAs have been very limited. Interviewed planning officials of the provincial administration and of the Provincial Department of Planning confirmed they do not have the full picture of private sector investments in their provinces. This is partly because, currently, much of the authority over private sector investment and licensing is still under line ministries who keep relevant data and have not systematically shared them with SNAs.

Data Management and Knowledge Solutions

For such a complicated reform like decentralization, learning by doing is key to ensure timely and targeting policy adjustment. After more than 2 decades of implementation, much knowledge and data have been produced about the decentralization reform in Cambodia. The data have been produced through the regular reporting system, while the knowledge has come from actual implementation and a range of pilot projects. The NCDD-S, for the interviews, has put efforts to collect those data in one place, both in a physical library and online.

However, the main problem is the fragmentation of data management, together with its limited sharing and use. For instance, the NCDD oversees 15 databases, including the annually updated CDB initiated in 2002 by Cambodia's Ministry of Planning. The CDB, featuring over 1,200 indicators, informs policymaking, like the 5-year plans, poverty rate calculations, and Cambodia Millennium Development Goals. Despite its usefulness, the CDB suffers from limited sharing, difficult accessibility, and skepticism about data quality. Nonetheless, it remains the sole large-scale local development dataset in Cambodia, with potential for improvement, citizen-generated data, and measuring CSDGs.[111]

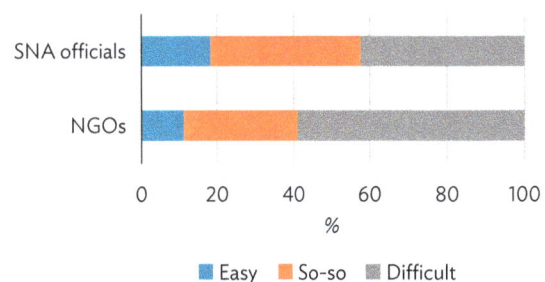

Figure 26: Perceived Convenience of Data Access

Q: If you need information/data relating to SNAs to perform your work, how easy is it to access?

NGO = nongovernment organization, SNA = subnational government.
Source: Authors' calculation based on the online surveys.

The study confirmed the difficulty of assessing data at the subnational level. As shown in Figure 26, 42% of SNAs and 59% of NGOs claimed it was difficult to get access to data about SNAs when they need them for their work, which includes reporting, collecting regular statistics, and program design. The interviewees attribute the challenges to the lack of broader awareness about the benefit of data sharing, uncertainty about rules and regulations on data sharing, and the intention of certain groups wanting to control data for their economic benefits and influence.

The challenges of data governance at the subnational level in Cambodia should not be viewed as an isolated issue, but rather as part of the wider e-government and data governance reform agenda. As mentioned earlier, the government is currently drafting an e-government policy specifically for SNAs. In this context, data is a crucial component for e-government operations at the SNA level, encompassing everything from routine administrative service delivery to more advanced initiatives like smart cities. Simultaneously, data governance at the SNA level must align with the broader national data governance framework, which, as depicted in Box 4, is still in its nascent stages and undergoing early reform.

Box 4: Data Governance in the Public Sector in Cambodia

Data governance in Cambodia is structured around two frameworks: four pillars and six elements. The four pillars encompass policy and legal framework, institutional framework, processes and procedures, and people and resources. Cambodia currently lacks a coherent policy and legal framework specific to data governance, which is critical for ensuring consistency and setting clear long-term objectives and measurable targets. While a macro institutional framework for digital transformation is in place, there is a lack of clarity in roles and coordination among stakeholders. The processes and procedures for data governance are less developed compared to those for statistical matters, and there are significant gaps in data classification, security, and privacy. Furthermore, there is a need for more human resources skilled in information and communication technology and data, as well as increased training and budget for relevant operations.

The six elements of data governance highlight specific areas such as data standardization and classification, data sharing and interoperability, data security, data privacy and ethics, digital identity, and data infrastructure. Cambodia faces challenges of standardizing and classifying data according to sensitivity and shareability. Data sharing and interoperability are limited due to unclear classifications and incompatible systems, despite promising initiatives like the Cambodia Data Exchange and CAMSTAT. In terms of data security, the government recognizes existing vulnerabilities and is working on policies and protocols, alongside establishing new agencies placed to be in charge of data securities. The country is in the early stages of developing measures for data privacy and ethics, with a low level of public and government awareness. Digital identity systems are yet to be integrated across government ministries, and the data infrastructure is still developing, with issues such as limited connectivity and the need for a common data storage solution. The government's approach envisions a hybrid cloud infrastructure, balancing centralized and decentralized elements.

Source: United Nations Department of Economic and Social Affairs. (Forthcoming). *Cambodia National Data Governance Baseline Report.*

Conclusions and Recommendations

Based on the detailed findings presented, this section presents specific conclusions and corresponding policy recommendations.

Awareness, Engagement, and Contributions of Subnational Administrations in the Cambodian Sustainable Development Goal Agenda

Conclusions

We have learned that Cambodia has committed to achieving the CSDGs. SNAs, in practice, have contributed to the CSDG agenda, but their voices and contributions have not been given sufficient attention in the CSDG documentation and VNR exercises. Low awareness and, more importantly, the lack of needed data have been the main challenges to systematic mapping and quantifying SNAs' contributions to the CSDG agenda.

Despite limited data and limited knowledge among surveyed SNA and CSO officials, those respondents see a high relevance of SNAs in the achievement of SDGs in Cambodia. Among the 18 CSDGs, SNAs and NGOs perceived that the former have contributed most to the CSDGs relating to reducing poverty, promoting health, gender equality, quality education, clean water, and hygiene; and promoting partnership. From citizens' perspectives, they expect that SNAs pay attention to quality education, followed by peace, justice, strong institutions, decent work and economic growth, and health.

Our qualitative research suggests that SNAs have contributed to all CSDGs, although there has not been enough quantitative data to quantify such contribution. At the same time, we also found patterns similar to those coming out of the surveys. First, SNAs have contributed more to peace, safety, and security, and to social sectors such as education, health, gender, and water supply, but less to the economic sectors, such as SME development, labor market, skills development, and natural resource management sector such as fisheries and forestry. SNAs will also need to take more responsibilities on emerging issues such as climate change considerations and preparedness for disasters triggered by natural hazards.

Recommendations

Raise awareness about the SDGs at SNAs using digital means. This should be done among SNA officials, citizens, and non-state actors. In addition to face-to-face training (which tends to be more costly and not necessarily effective), quality digital content should be produced and disseminated through social media and online training.

Better engage SNAs in the planned activity for the next CSDG exercises. In the past, due to time constraints and other logistical challenges, very few SNAs were directly consulted on questions relating to CSDGs. It is recommended that time for SNA engagement be factored into future exercises. Also, to partly overcome the cost and time constraints, online surveys and online discussions with SNAs should be used.

Develop and analyze dataset on SDGs and SNAs. Significant data have been generated both at the national and subnational levels. However, fragmentation and data sharing have been limited, resulting in much data being left unused. Relevant datasets should be developed using existing data and made ready for the next rounds of CSDG monitoring (and other M&E rounds).

The Four Dimensions of the Cambodian Sustainable Development Goal Localizations at Subnational Administration Level

Conclusions

Despite much progress, the legal, policy, and institutional frameworks on SNAs in Cambodia have come to a point where consistency and coordination have become critical. There have been many laws, regulations, and policies that seek to define and reform the organizational structure, functions, resources, partnership, and accountability of SNAs. However, there are still gaps in key aspects such as on functional assignments, partnerships with the private sector, and M&E. Even more challenging is the consistency and coordination among key laws, rules, and policies. Not addressing these challenges will lead the whole reform effort into a logjam situation; SNAs' ability to contribute to national development priorities and, by extension, to the CSDG achievement, will be undermined.

As far as contributing to the SDG achievement is concerned, SNAs have been given bigger budgets in the last decade. However, vertical and horizontal imbalances remain a key challenge, together with limited own-source revenue. The functional assignment process needs urgent attention for both policy and implementation, especially at the DMK level, where many functions are expected to be transferred. Finally, SNA planning needs further streamlining and better use of data so that SNA resources and efforts can be better aligned with the national development priority and thus the CSDGs.

As Cambodia is a unitary state, SNAs are considered a part of the government's broader check-and-balance system, but with their own specific autonomy. Democratic accountability mechanisms have been built int the structure of the SNAs. At the subnational level, while mechanisms of political representation still exist, no real political competition is observed. The SNA governance system also has built-in mechanisms for civic engagement. Other accountability mechanisms have been developed and improved over time. However, key gaps remain. For instance, data storage, sharing, and use have become urgent challenges in the current SNA reporting exercise. Internal audit functions at SNAs have yet to be developed and external audits on SNAs have rarely been done.

Recommendations

Improve coordination by more effective use of the new reform coordination mechanisms (i.e., the Reform 3+1 mechanism).[112] Moving forward, it is critical that the newly established Secretariat on Reform 3+1 be strengthened and used to coordinate the decentralization reform with the PFMRP, NPAR, and the judicial reform.

---

[112]   This refers to the coordination among the decentralization, PFMRP, NPAR, and judicial reform.

This mechanism should also be used to bring line ministries to get their commitment and impose accountability with regard to sector functional transfer.

Strengthen the collaboration between the NCDD-S, MEF, MOI, MCS, and MOP. Complementing the participation expected to be generated through the Reform 3+1 mechanism, efficiency in moving things forward can be achieved by having key actors working closely together. Those actors, among others, are the NCDD-S, MEF, MOI, MCS, and MOP. These are central agencies with sufficient leverages to pull other line ministries into the reform momentum.

Establish explicit and systematic linkages between SNA functions and CSDGs, backed up by available data. In the current context of reform fragmentation and, at times, confusion, making explicit and systematic the connections between SNAs roles and works with each CSDG can usher in a new sense of responsibility, harmonization, and joint accountability. The cross-agency coordination can be further enhanced with concrete quantifiable and verifiable data and evidence.

Make the functional transfer to the DMKs an urgent matter. The persistently small budget of the DM, despite some increases, raised concerns with regard to service delivery. Improvement of budget allocation to the DM level will be necessary for improving public service delivery. This should be done along with the process of clarifying obligatory versus permissive functions for the 55 functions and the costing of specific functions.

Improve the working relationship between the DM and line department. This can be done by identifying relevant sector regulations that need to be revised to be in line with the D&D reform, ensuring that line departments factor in the recent functional transfer in their regular planning and budgeting exercises, and addressing the inconsistency in the use of data for planning and M&E purposes by the DM administrations versus the line departments.

Systematize the ways SNAs can work with the private sector. This can be done by encouraging SNA administrations to set up clear mechanisms for coordinating and working closely with the private sector and updated data on private sector engagement in local service delivery and development.

Appendixes

Appendix 1: The Process and Criteria for Reviewing the Cambodian Sustainable Development Goals in Cambodia[1]

Based on the experience of the 2019 Voluntary National Review and due to the impact of the coronavirus disease (COVID-19) outbreak, Cambodia made adjustment to the Cambodian Sustainable Development Goals (CSDGs) and those that are relevant in the National Strategic Development Plan. The review process started in July 2020 with the Ministry of Planning (MOP) requesting line ministries and agencies to consider adjusting their sector indicators, especially those that do not have supporting data, and review indicators that do not meet the target and consider some indicators that may highlight efforts of agencies to contribute to achieving the CSDGs. In February 2021, due to the seriousness of the COVID-19 outbreak, the MOP further instructed line ministries and relevant agencies to also reflect the impact of the pandemic into their efforts to reach the CSDG targets.

After receiving recommendations from line ministries and agencies on the draft list, the MOP organized a high-level meeting on 30 November 2021 to review and approve the final draft. To ensure that all comments from line ministries and agencies and stakeholders are included in the document, the MOP sent the final draft to the line ministries and relevant agencies for final review. The draft of the revised CSDG was approved on 1 July 2022.

Seven points or criteria were used to guide the revision:

- Adjustments must be based on the results of the CSDGs, as shown in the Progress Report 2019 of the Achievement of the CSDGs, focusing on non-supportive data indicators (13 equals 8.78%) and performance indicators.
- Consider excluding (or seeking support data sources) for indicators that do not have support data sources.
- Modify indicators (including meeting the conditions of the indicators) so that they can be implemented and have supporting data sources.
- Adjust the milestones by increasing or decreasing them based on the actual situation (including the effects of the COVID-19 spread) that can be achieved.
- Edit data cycles based on data collection cycle such as the Cambodian Socio-Economic Survey.
- Focus on areas where indicators do not have supporting data sources or have performance indicators below the set targets.
- Consider adding new indicators to demonstrate the efforts of line ministries and agencies to contribute to the achievement of the CSDGs.

---

[1]   (MOP, 2022a).

Appendix 2: Key Laws and Regulations
on Subnational Administrations in Cambodia

Overall SNA governance and reform

Law on the Management of Capital, provincial, municipals, districts, and Khan (2008)
Law on the Management of Commune/Sangkat Administration (2001)

On functional assignment

Sub-decree #68 on the General Process of Transferring Functions and Resources to SNA (2012)
Sub-decree #285 on the Selection, Management and Implementation of Permissive Functions by SNA Councils (2014)
Sub-decree #68 on the Provision of Administrative Services by SNA (2013)
Sub-decree #18 on the Establishment of OWSO for Administrative Service Provision at SNA (2017)
Sub-decree #18 on the Establishment of Ombudsman Office at SNA (2017)
Various sub-decrees and Prakas on the transfer of specific functions to SNAs

On fiscal decentralization

Law on Financial Regime and the Management of Property of SNA (2011)
Sub-decree #6 on the Transfer for Conditional Grant to SNA (2017)
Sub-decree #36 on the Establishment and Functioning of the DMF (2012)
Sub-decree #172 on the Financial Management System of DM administrations (2012)

On public financial management at SNA

Law on Financial Regime and the Management of Property of SNA (2011)
Law on Public Procurement (2012) and various sub-decree, Prakas and Guideline on public procurement at SNA level
Sub-decree #219 on the Development Plan and 3 Year Investment Plan for CP and DMK (2009)

On personnel management and capacity development at SNA

Policy on the management and development of human resource at SNA (2013),
Law on separate statute for personnel at SNA (2016),
Sub-decree #240 on the delegation of authority to Capital, provincial and municipalities in managing personnel working at sub-national level (2017)
Sub-decree #114 on the Organizational Structure and Positions in Line Ministries and Sub-National Administration (2017)
Sub-decree #192 on the Establishment of National School on Local Administration (2016)

Source: Compiled by the authors.

Appendix 3: Key Government Agencies for Decentralization Reform in Cambodia

The **National Committee for Subnational Democratic Development and its Secretariat (NCDD-S)** is a cross-government agency, formally established by royal decree in December 2008 to coordinate and lead the implementation of the Organic Law.[2] The NCDD-S has 16 members and is chaired by the minister of interior with two deputy chairs, one of which is the minister of economy and finance. Other members are at levels of minister and state secretary. The NCDD-S establishes subcommittees on functions and resources, financial and fiscal affairs, planning, and personnel administration. The NCDD-S has various units including a Policy Analysis and Development Division, a Monitoring and Evaluation and Information Division, a Program Management and Support Division, and an Administration and Finance Division.

The **Ministry of Interior (MOI)** has two main parts: the civil administration and the national police. The MOI also supervises the performance of subnational administrations (SNAs), supports central government efforts to build their capacity, and plays a lead role in addressing any irregularities committed by SNAs. In some cases, the MOI can facilitate the dismissal of councilors. It also plays a key role in the appointments of governors; boards of governors; deputy governors; and directors of administration, clerks, and finance directors at subnational administration levels. The MOI also chairs some important subcommittees of the NCDD and provides the bulk of staff of the secretariat.

The **Ministry of Economy and Finance (MEF)** is a powerful central ministry overseeing all budgetary and public financial management matters. As provided in Sub-decree #488 (2013) and its later revision, the MEF has many general departments, two of which are particularly relevant here. The first is the General Department of Budget, which has departments in charge of budget formulation, budget execution, and investment. The other is the General Department of Sub-National Finance, which has one department for Capital and Provincial financial management, one for District and Municipality, and one for Commune and Sangkat level. At the subnation level, it has (i) the Provincial Department of Economy and Finance (PDEF), (ii) provincial customers and exercise branch, (iii) provincial and district taxation branch, and (iv) Provincial Treasury.[3] The MEF operates mainly through the PDEF, which serves as the financial controller over the revenue and spending of various technical line departments and SNAs. The PDEF also plays important roles in managing procurement works of those spending agencies. The MEF, through PDEF, is also in charge of periodic capacity-building activities (mainly in form of cascade training on specific guidelines) for subnational level.

The **Ministry of Civil Service (MCS)** works to support and coordinate personnel transfer, management, and capacity building of human resources under the National Program for Sub-national Democratic Development. Working as a key member of the NCDD, MCS drafts relevant policies, laws, sub-decrees, and regulations. It is also a key player in planning and monitoring key aspects of personnel management including wage. At the subnational level, MCS performs these roles through its Provincial Department of Civil Service.

The **Ministry of Planning (MOP)** is a key member of the NCDD responsible for leading the drafting and adoption of key policy and regulation on planning at SNA. At the subnational level, MOP has a Provincial Department of Planning, which assists in the management, analysis, and production of necessary local development data (such as the provincial scorecard) to be used by SNAs in developing their annual development plan and 3-year Investment Plan.

---

[2]   Royal Government of Cambodia (RGC) (2008) The establishment and functioning of the NCDD.
[3]   RGC (2013).

Line ministries and their deconcentrated offices have important roles in facilitating the process of functional assignment to SNAs. Virtually all line ministries are members of the NCDD and are required to establish their own working groups on deconcentration and decentralization (directly led by the minister or a secretary of state) to support development of policy and to implement agreed reforms. Line ministries have been subject to more rigorous deconcentration reforms in the last decade. As of now, all line departments are considered budget entities with their own budget and have spending authority. However, such deconcentration has happened not in all but only selected priority ministries, especially education and health.

The **National School of Local Administration (NASLA).** NASLA was established in 2016 for "building capacity for civil servants, council of sub-national administrations, students, and other stakeholders as well as conducting research on governance, local development, enhancement of local autonomy and management of sub-national administration." NASLA started providing training programs in 2018 and its role will be even more important especially for building the capacity of district, municipality, and khan personnel, including the newly transferred personnel.

Appendix 4: One Window Service Units and One Window Service Offices

The One Window Service Office (OWSO) and One Window Service Unit (OWSU) are two main mechanisms for delivering administrative services to citizens and businesses and generating nontax revenues for subnational administrations (SNAs). Their establishment and functioning are provided in Sub-decree #18 (2017); Sub-decree #25 (2020); and various Prakas, circulars, and instructions. At the national level, the Ministry of Interior, especially the Department of Functions and Resource, plays an essential supporting role for both OWSU and OSWO. OWSO and OWSU also receive close attention and support from the deputy prime minister and minister of interior. Because OWSO and OWSU also generate nontax revenue, their operations and management are also subject to critical regulations issued by the Ministry of Economy and Finance, especially the General Department of State Asset and Non-Tax Revenue. Since early 2020, specific reforms and progress have been made to OWSO and OWSU, as detailed below.

Since early 2020, OWSO at the District, Municipality, and Khan (DMK) level has gone through some critical organizational and procedural changes. The first is the physical office's readjustment in line with the government's reintegration of all line offices to be under DMK administrations. This move has further institutionalized the OWSO and the district office to the overall DMK administrative structure. It thus establishes clearer and more official accountability lines been OWSO heads and staff with DMK councils and the Board of Governors. The second change is the adoption of a new Prakas (#751), followed by the guideline on the Principles and Procedures for Service Delivery at the DMK OWSO. This change seeks to align and clarify the OWSO operation in line with the recent organizational changes. The Prakas and the guideline seek to clearly outline the organizational structure, physical office arrangement, equipment needs, roles and responsibilities of key actors, and specific steps in OWSO service delivery process. It also provides various appendixes on sample logos, forms, and reporting templates.

OWSU, although formally established only in 2017, has made speedy progress as compared to OWSO. After Sub-decree #18 was adopted in 2017, a Prakas on OWSU was adopted in the same year. The Guideline on the Process and Procedures for Service Delivery by OWSU was adopted in 2018. Since 2018, the service delivery functions by OWSU have been implemented and expanded rapidly. As of early 2020, based on the data provided by MOI, OWSU provided about 559 services, divided into 14 sectors. Because of its high revenue volume, the government in 2020 took a quick step to adopt a sub-decree (#25) to ensure effective management of its budget, including incentive sharing.

Overall, the number of services provided by OWSU has slightly decreased between 2019 and 2020. However, the revenue collected increased. The drop in the overall number of services (of about 6%) was due to the drop in the number of administrative services, legalization services, and labor-related services. However, there was an increase in the case for construction and land titling, agricultural activity permits, and public work and transport (vehicle number plates). On the other hand, the total revenue collected increased by about 66%, thanks mainly to the increase in the service fees from construction and land titling, agriculture, and public works.

In term of governance, since early 2020, several changes have been made. The first was the adoption of Sub-decree #25 (briefly mentioned earlier), followed by the adoption of other key regulatory documents to manage OWSU revenue better. These legal documents help clarify the procedures for delivering specific sector services, build staff capacity and expand the presence of OWSU to all the 25 Capital and Provinces. Much effort has also been made on promoting information and communication technology and e-governance.

References

Asian Development Bank (ADB). 2021. *Country Snapshot on SDG Localization in Asia and the Pacific - Conceptual Framework.*

———. 2023. *Asian Development Outlook September 2023.*

Association of Sub-National Administration Council (ASAC). 2023. *Voluntary Subnational Review - Cambodia.*

Bhatti, Z., and L. McDonald. 2020. *Deepening Decentralization Within Centrally Led States: The Direction of Local Governance Reform in Southeast Asia.* World Bank.

Datareportal. 2023. *Digital 2022 Cambodia.* https://datareportal.com/reports/digital-2022-cambodia.

Global Road Safety Facility. 2021. *Road Safety Data Review in Cambodia.*

International Monetary Fund (IMF). 2001. *Annex to Chapter 6: Classification of the Functions of Government.*

———. 2022. *2022 Article IV Consultation.* Press release, staff report, and statement by the Executive Director for Cambodia.

Kaufmann, D. A. K. and M. Mastruzz. 2020. *The Worldwide Governance Indicators.* World Bank.

Ministry of Economy and Finance (MEF). 2018, 2019, 2020, 2021, 2022, 2023. *Budget in Brief for 2018, 2019, 2020, 2021, 2022, 2023.*

———. 2019. *SNA Budget System Reform Strategy (SNA-BSRS) 2010-2025.*

———. 2022a. *Additional Information on SNA Budget for 2022.*

———. 2022b. *Instruction #2 on the Use of FMIS at the Capital and Provincial Administration.*

———. 2022c. *Instruction #4 on the Use of FMIS Portal at DM and CS Level.*

Ministry of Education, Youth, and Sport (MEYS). 2023. *Prakas No. 1065 on the Transfer of Education Personnel to DMK Administrations.*

Ministry of Industry, Science, Technology, and Innovation (MISTI). 2014. *Prakas #461 on the Procedures for Issuing, Changing, Extending, Suspending, and Withdrawing Licenses of Private Water Supply Operators.*

Ministry of Interior (MOI). 2018. *The Implementation of Social Services at CS Level.*

MOI and Ministry of Planning (MOP). 2020. *PK #0149 on the Additional Guideline on the Develpment of the 3-Year Investment Program for CP, DMK and CS.*

MOP. 2012. *Scorecard of the Implementation of the CMDG at Sub-national Level in 2012: Based on CDB.*

———. 2022a. *CSDG 2016–2030: Revised List of Targets and Indicators by Goals.*

———. 2022b. *Mid-term Review 2021 of the NSDP 2019–2023 Implementation.*

———. 2023. *Cambodia's VNR: Accelerating the Recovery from COVID-19 and the Full Implementation of the 2030 Agenda.*

Ministry of Women's Affairs. 2020. *Neary Rattanak V (2019–2023).*

National Committee for Sub-National Democratic Development (NCDD). 2021. *National Program on Sub-National Democratic Development (NP-SNDD) for 2021–2030.*

National Committee for Sub-National Democratic Development and its Secretariat (NCDD-S). 2022. *National Committee for Sub-National Democratic Development.* Retrieved from https://ncdd.gov.kh/projects/.

———. 2023. *Findings on the Management and Implementation of Education Functions Transferred to DMK Administration.*

National Institute of Statistics (NIS). 2020. *National Population Census in 2019.*

———. 2021. *Cambodian Socio-economic Survey (CSES).*

Organisation for Economic Co-operation and Development/United Cities and Local Government. 2022. *World Observatory on Subnational Government Finance and Investment - Key Findings.*

Royal Government of Cambodia (RGC). 1995a. *Regulation on Public Accounting Rules.*

———. 1995b. *Regulation on Public Expenditure Control.*

———. 2000. *Law on Audit.*

———. 2008. *Law on Administrative Management of the Capital, Provinces, Municipalities.*

———. 2011. *National Policy on Spatial Planning.*

———. 2013. *Policy on the Management and Development of Human Resource at SNA.*

———. 2016. *National Social Protection Policy Framework (2016–2025).*

———. 2017. *Sub-decree no. 18 on the Establishment of One-Window Service Mechanisms at SNA.*

———. 2018, 2019, 2020, 2021, 2022, 2023. *Budget Laws for 2018, 2019, 2020, 2021, 2022, 2023.*

———. 2019a. *Rectangular Strategy Phase IV.*

———. 2019b. *Sub-decree No. 182, 183, 184 on the Functional Transfers to DMK Adminsitrations.*

———. 2021a. *Cambodia Digital Economy and Society Policy Framework 2021–2035.*

———. 2021b. *Policy on Safe Communes and Villages.*

———. 2021c. *Strategic Framework and Program for Cambodia's Economic Recovery (2021–2023).*

———. 2021d. *Urban Solid Waste Management Policy 2020–2030.*

———. 2022a. *Digital Government Policy.*

———. 2022b. *Law on Non-Tax Revenue.*

———. 2022c. *Strategy for the Three Reform Coordination.*

———. 2023a. *Cambodia's Voluntary National Review (VNR) 2023: Accelerating the Recovery from the Coronavirus disease (COVID-19) and the Full Implementation of the 2030 Agenda.*

———. 2023b. *Law on Public Procurement.*

———. 2023c. *Law on Taxation.*

———. 2023d. *Public Finance System Law.*

———. 2023e. *Sub-decree No. 213 on the Transfer of Functions on Education Sector to DMK Administration.*

———. 2023f. *Summary of the 2024 Draft Law.*

———. 2023g. *The Pentagonal Strategy Phase 1.*

Roberts, D. 2003. From 'Communism' to 'Democracy' in Cambodia: A Decade of Transition and Beyond. *Communist and Post-Communist Studies.* 36 (2): 245–258.

The Asia Foundation (TAF). 2022. *A Diagnostic Study on the Policy Process and Use of Data: The Case of Cambodia and Insights from ASEAN.*

United Nations Department of Economic and Social Affairs. (Forthcoming). *Cambodia National Data Governance Baseline Report.*

UN Development Programme, Australian Aid, MEF. 2021. *2021 COVID-19 Economic and Social Impact Assessment in Cambodia - An Integrated Modelling Approach.*

World Bank. 2017. *Cambodia: Sustainable Strong Growth for the Benefit of All.*

———. 2020. *Cambodia Economic Update: Restrained Recovery.* Retrieved from World Bank.

———. 2022a. *Cambodia Poverty Assessment - Toward a More Inclusive and Resilient Cambodia.*

———. 2022b. *Cambodia's Intergovernmental Architecture.*

———. 2022c. *NTR System in Cambodia.*

———. 2023. Macroeconomic and Fiscal Model (MFMod).

World Bank and TAF. 2013. *Voice, Choice, and Decision: A Study of Local Basic Service Delivery in Cambodia.*